Becoming Buddha

Buddhist Contemplative Psychology
in a Western Context

Becoming Buddha: Buddhist Contemplative Psychology in a
Western Context

ISBN: 978-1-7350112-1-9

Published by Bright Alliance

First Edition

Printed and Bound in the United States of America

Layout and design by Brad Reynolds integralartandstudies.com

For more information on John Churchill see: samadhiintegral.com

Becoming Buddha

Buddhist Contemplative Psychology in a Western Context

John Churchill, Psy.D.

BRIGHT
ALLIANCE

Table of Contents

CHAPTER ONE A WESTERN CONTEXT 1

CHAPTER TWO: BUDDHIST CONTEMPLATIVE
        PSYCHOLOGY 15

   The Three Turnings of the Dharma 17

   The First Turning of the Teaching:
     The Lesser Vehicle 19

   The Second Turning of the Teaching:
     The Great Vehicle 37

   The Third Turning of the Teaching:
     The Buddha-Nature Vehicle 41

CHAPTER THREE BUDDHIST ESSENCE PSYCHOLOGY 47

   Mahamudra 49

   The Path of Development in Mahamudra 53

   sGam po pa's Four-Yoga Model 57

   Mahamudra and Brain Research 67

   rDzogchen 72

   Classifications of rDzogchen 72

   The A Khrid System of rDzogchen 76

   The Three Bodies 92

   The Five Primordial Wisdoms 93

Bibliography 101

Becoming Buddha

Buddhist Contemplative Psychology
in a Western Context

CHAPTER ONE

A WESTERN CONTEXT

$\mathscr{I}$t has been estimated by the World Health organization that 25% of people worldwide will suffer from a mental disorder. This means at this moment in time approximately 450 million people are suffering from a psychological disease. To make matters worse, due to stigma, fear of discrimination, and lack of access to mental health providers, it is believed that two-thirds of those with a psychological disorder will suffer in silence and never seek help (Mental Disorders, 2001).

Starting near the beginning of the 20th century with Sigmund Freud and the development of psychoanalysis, the field of clinical psychology has creatively evolved in its attempt to reduce and eliminate mental and emotional suffering (Weston, 1998). Its successful evolution has expanded to include hundreds of different theoretical and therapeutic orientations grouped under such broad categories as psychodynamic, cognitive, behavioral, systemic, and humanistic psychology. Research has shown that many of these approaches are successful in treating disorders such as anxiety, depression and others (Seligman, 1995).

As biological science also evolved, major developments in psychotropic medications began to address psychological disorders at a biological level. With the introduction of Lithium in the 1950's, followed by the developments of a series of anti-psychotics, Valium in the 1960's, Prozac in the late 1980's, and the popularization of Ritalin in the 1990's there has been a continued development of drug treatments for a wide range of disorders (Ingersoll & Rak, 2015). By 2010, in the United States more than one in five adults was on at least one psychotropic medication, with more than a quarter of the adult female population on these drugs (Medco, 2011).

Despite all the developments in psychotherapy and psychopharmacology in the United States, there has been no reduction in the prevalence of mental disease, and at present 43.8 million adults, or 18.5% of the population, experiences a mental illness in a given year (Mental Health Among Adults, 2015). According to the New Economics Foundation, the United States, despite all its wealth and the psychological services at the disposal of its population, is unable to offer sustainable wellness for its population and only ranks 108/140 in happiness (Happy Planet Index, 2016). Aside from improving access to treatment and training many more professionals, there is reason to wonder what else might reduce the extent of mental disease and the lack of human flourishing.

Clinical psychology as practiced in North America has been criticized as a product of "WEIRD" (Western, educated, industrialized, rich, and democratic) societies (Christopher, Wendt, Marecek, & Goodman 2014). It has been argued that it is too easy for modern psychologists to fail to recognize the priority given to western cultural constructs. As a product of WEIRD, western psychology can be seen as folk psychology, situated squarely in a paradigm of scientific modernity (Brunner, 1990). Post-modern psychologists have argued that the science of psychology is not as objective as it is often believed to be (Gergon, 2001; Pickering, 2006). Its training and practices transmit a set of cultural beliefs concerning a moral vision that defines what constitutes emotional and cognitive health, and the good life (Christopher, 1996, 1999). For instance, Western psychology asserts the primacy of the mind versus the body, individuality versus community, and the dominance of the scientific materialist worldview despite the evidence from quantum physics that mind is as fundamental as matter (Smethham, 2010). This unrecognized paradigm features prominently in North American professional discourse surrounding psychological and behavioral health.

One avenue to begin addressing the vast unmet need for psychological intervention is to adopt an attitude of cultural humility and re-envision psychotherapy as a global human science (Tervalon, & Murray-Garcia 1998). This means recognizing and studying those dismissed non-Western psychologies that offer important perspectives on the human condition (Segall, Lonner & Berry, 1998). These under-utilized resources can help in the development of useful clinical and behavioral applications to reduce suffering and support the growth of happiness.

One such psychological framework is contemplative psychology, the distillation of the psychological understanding of the world religious traditions (De Witt & Baird, 1991). Underneath the cultural packaging of mysticism, myth, religion, and ritual is a psychological science, a body of knowledge that can be actualized in the laboratory of each person's mind (Wilber 2007). The deeper structure of these contemplative practices, as is found in Buddhist and Hindu traditions, appears to follow a universal stage-by-stage progression, while the realizations of each stage are themselves influenced by the theological, cultural, and philosophical particularities of each tradition (Brown 1986; Diperna, 2015).

Beginning with the 1902 publication of William James's *The Varieties of Religious Experience*, the study of contemplative psychology as a legitimate field of study in Western Psychology has unfolded slowly over the last century. The exploration of cross-cultural contemplative practices, for instance, was important for Carl Jung, the eminent Swiss psychoanalyst and his students of Analytical Psychology (Odajnk, 1993). Meditation slowly became a more serious a part of an American psychological inquiry in the 1950's with the exploration of Zen Buddhism by a number of psychoanalysts (Jung, 1939; Fromm, E., Suzuki, D.T.

& De Martino, R. (1960); DeMartino, R. (1991). The interest in meditation led to the popularization of Transcendental Meditation (TM), a modernization of the Hindu Raja Yoga meditation tradition (Desmarais, 2008). It was the TM practitioners who were first studied by the Harvard Cardiologist Herbert Benson. His research into the reversal of the fight/flight stress response then led to the first popular secularization of meditation: the relaxation response (Benson, 1974).

At present the majority of contemplative interventions originate from the Buddhist tradition (Shonin, Van Gordon & Griffiths, 2013, 2014). This is likely due to a number of factors. Buddhism is a non-theistic tradition (Wallace, 2007). It does not necessarily rely upon a metaphysical understanding of human experience and is built upon the humanistic concern of reducing and extinguishing human suffering (Young-Eisendrath, 2008), and can be understood pragmatically without the need for metaphysics (Batchelor, 1998). As a meditation discipline it values objective truth and is more aligned with the values of science than those of pure belief (Dalai Lama, 2005). The Dalai Lama, arguably the most influential Buddhist teacher in the world, has been in dialogue with neuroscientists, psychologists, and quantum physicists for decades. He wrote in 2005:

> If scientific analysis were conclusively to demonstrate certain claims in Buddhism to be false, then we must accept the findings of science and abandon those claims. (Dalai Lama, 2005, p. 2-3).

The foundation of Buddhist thought is psychological. A psychology that is found in the Abidharma, the phenomenological study of cognition and perception of early Buddhism (Govinda, 1974). Abidharma was developed through the use of meditative stability to investigate the first person experience of psychological processes (Markic, & Kordes, 2016). The maps and models, developed by generations of meditators, have a precision similar to those developed in cognitive psychology (Lancaster, 1997), and are likewise similar in their understanding of the complex relationship between thoughts, feelings and behavior (Segal, 2003).

The tradition of Buddhist contemplative psychology has become popular in the West in the form of secular mindfulness meditation. In the 1970's

Jon Kabat-Zinn, a trained Buddhist contemplative teacher and molecular biologist, developed a program designed to reduce psychological stress in chronically ill patients as they received health care. This new program, Mindfulness Based Stress Reduction (MBSR) was a melding of different Buddhist approaches including Zen, Tibetan Essence traditions, and Burmese modernist Insight meditation into a simple contemplative practice (McMahan, 2008). MBSR brought meditation out of obscurity and into hospitals, schools, and businesses. Today, over 20 million Americans (6.5% of the population) practice some form of meditation (Elias, 2009), and in the United Kingdom 25% of the population (Mental Health Foundation, 2010). This interest in meditation is now influencing a growing research effort in academia. In 2012, 500 scientific papers were published on the topic of mindfulness alone. This compares to only 50 papers per annum a decade previously. The research science indicates that the contemplative practices of concentration, mindfulness, compassion, and loving kindness have a profound impact on the brain (Hölzel, Lazar, Gard, Schuman-Olivier, Vago, & Ott, 2011). So much so, that a wholly new multi-disciplinary field of contemplative neuroscience is developing (Davidson, 2012).

At this point in the integration of contemplative and clinical psychologies, Buddhist derived interventions (BDIs) span the therapeutic range, and are used to treat a range of psychological disorders including schizophrenia-spectrum disorders (Johnson, Penn, Fredrickson, Kring, Meyer, Catalino, & Brantley, 2011), personality disorders (Soler, Feliu-Soler, Pascual, Portella, Martin-Blanco, & Pérez, 2012), substance abuse disorders (Witkiewitz, Bowen, Douglas, & Hsu, 2013), mood disorders (Hofmann, Sawyer, Witt, & Oh, 2010), anxiety disorders (Vollestad, Nielson, & Nielson, 2012) and depression (Teasdale, Segal, Williams, Ridgeway, Soulsby, & Lau, 2000).

As the interest in contemplative practices has developed over the last 20 years and moved into mainstream culture there is concern among pioneers in the field that consumer culture is unjustly and unwisely appropriating mindfulness (Cosgrove, 2013). Rather than being deeply researched and understood as an approach to reduce for human suffering, "McMindfulness," an oversimplified versions of contemplative practice, could just become another commodity for sale and dispensed in a weekend workshop (Hyland, 2015).

Some believe that simply teaching present-centered awareness without the systematic cultivation of compassion and ethics is not aligned with the original teachings and easily obscures the depth of psychological transformation that the Buddhist contemplative psychology has to offer (Harrington & Dunne 2015; Monteiro, Musten, & Compson, 2015; Purser, 2015; Purser & Milillo, 2015). They argue that the dominance of secular mindfulness approaches in the research and in the proliferation of Buddhist-derived interventions (BDI) in psychotherapy, coupled with the field's unconscious folk bias towards a modernist, individualistic, Cartesian worldview has led Buddhist contemplative psychology to be selectively and simplistically appropriated. Ift contemplative psychology is only viewed through the lens of scientific and humanistic psychology then it cannot be understood. Psychology directs its understanding of the normal by drawing upon knowledge of the abnormal and pathological. However, Buddhist contemplative psychology is soteriological, a path of liberation; it is directed to the supernormal human potential, Buddhahood, and draws upon the understanding of normal functioning to enhance the path towards the fruition of human potential (Lancaster, 2007).

Contemplative psychology and its rich pathways toward emotional stability, cognitive peace, clarity, and optimal altruistic living has not been approached as a system in its entirety. One consequence of this is the poverty of literature outlining the larger psychological context of these practices and the significant and permanent potential benefits they can bring to psychological development and the alleviation of suffering (Loizzo, 2014). What exists now is, arguably, a superficial clinical practice paradigm.

This theoretical study will explore Buddhist contemplative psychology as presented within the non-sectarian presentation of the Indo-Tibetan Mahamudra and rDzogchen tradition (Brown, 2006; Chagmé, 1997; Klonchen-pa, 1993). Mahamudra and RDzogchen will be examined because many, including the Dalai Lama, believe these parallel systems to be the pinnacle understanding of Buddhist contemplative psychology (Lama, 2000: see also; Chagmé, 1997; Ponlop, 2003). This approach integrates the three main developments of Buddhist psychological thought, Hinyana, Mahayana, and Vajrayana (Ray, 2002), into a single progressive system of psychological development and practice (Guenther, 1989). These three approaches to contemplative psychology are best seen as three phases or empirical revolutions that sequentially build upon each prior discovery (Brown, 2016).

The objective of this research is to support the filling of the gap in the literature and to support building a better conceptual bridge that integrates Buddhist and Western understandings of psychological development. This will allow psychologists and interested meditators a deeper understanding of practice, provide a more complete theoretical understanding of the psychological transformative process that a meditator might undergo, and support therapists' and their clients' contemplative exploration beyond introductory mindfulness practices towards greater freedom from psychological suffering and the flowering of human potential.

TRANSLITERATION

To assist the reader in referencing Tibetan terms I have used the Tibetan transliteration method refined in

1959 by Turrell Wylie. This method has subsequently become a standard transliteration scheme in Tibetan studies, especially in the Western world. Wylie does not try to give pronunciation hints and serves only to accurately reproduce written Tibetan. As such diacritical marks used to mark sounds are not in this text for either Tibetan (Tbt) or Sanskrit (Skt).

CHAPTER TWO

BUDDHIST CONTEMPLATIVE PSYCHOLOGY

The tradition of Buddhist contemplative psychology originates with the great Indian sage Siddhartha Gautama. Siddhartha Gautama, or Shakyamuni Buddha, as he was to become known, was born around 563 B.C.E. at Lumbini in the foothills of the Himalayan range (Cousins, & Bechert, 1996). He was a prince of the Northern Indian Shakya kingdom and a member of the royal warrior caste, the *kshatriya*. It is believed that he was an intelligent and strong young man and received the best education of the day, mastering the arts, and sciences, including the martial arts and strategy (Powers, 2009). At 16 years of age he was married and continued to enjoy the comforts of palace life and the pleasures of the royal life style until he renounced his life of privilege to seek an answer to his deep existential questioning. According to Buddhist hagiography, his quest was initiated after the idyllic life in the court of his father King Shuddhodhana was shattered by exposure to the realities of old age, sickness, and death outside the glamor and manufactured reality of the capital's palace at Kapilavastu (Rahula, 1974).

Siddhartha became a forest dweller and joined the ascetic srama movement of the day, studying and mastering the meditative systems of Arada Kalama, and Rudraka Ramputra (Yogi, 2001). It is said that upon displaying mastery of each of these systems the respective masters suggested that he teach. But Siddhartha, despite the meditative absorptions he had mastered, had not answered his quest to understand human suffering so he continued on his own. His 6-year quest culminated at Bodhgaya, under the shade of a large sacred fig tree (ficus religiosa) on the banks of the Nairanjana River. It was there after a 49-day period of intense meditation that he is said to have had a permanent psychological transformation, the extinction of all causes of psychological suffering, nirvana, and the realization of anuttarasamyak-sambodhi, enlightenment.

This realization led to a teaching career that spanned four and a half decades until the Buddha's death at the age of 80. The teaching of Shakyamuni Buddha initiated the development of the Buddhist tradition. This tradition became a force of civilization in the world, a culture, system of ethics, monasticism, philosophy, psychology, and training specifically designed to bring about the realization of the highest reaches of human development, leadership and heroic altruism (Ray, 1999).

THE THREE TURNINGS OF THE DHARMA

Through the view of the Indo-Tibetan Tradition, Buddhism has evolved through three major stages of evolution, or turnings of the wheel of the dharma. Similar to fundamental paradigm shifts seen in other forms of science (Kuhn, 1970), this evolutionary process, here into the causes of human existential unhappiness, is easiest understood as a progression of understanding with each stage supported by the cognitive and metacognitive findings of the prior stage. Whilst the tradition maintains that Shakyamuni (c. 480 BCE – 400 BCE) taught all three turnings during his lifetime, and that a minority who had a greater capacity for a more sophisticated path initially practiced the latter two phases of the teaching, it is believed that understanding of the later turnings evolved as the cultural environment became more open to their innovations. In that way the tradition is seen to have evolved through time as more people developed capacity, whilst at the same time recognizing that the later teachings were always a part of the tradition.

The growth of Buddhist psychology was dependent upon the development of what the cognitive psychologist Jean Piaget referred to as the psychological capacity for formal operational thinking. The formal operational stage of cognition allows for the capacity for abstract thought: the use of hypothetical and deductive reasoning to reflect upon situations that are not present in concrete reality (Piaget, 1972). This stage of cognition includes the ability to problem solve in a logical and methodical way, and metacognition: the important psychological capacity to monitor and think about one's own thought processes. With the capacity for causal analysis and self-reflection available at this level of cognitive complexity, teachings could be developed that focused on understanding the cause and effect of the pervasive reactivity characteristic of the undeveloped mind. With a foundation in causal analysis, Buddhist contemplative thought then evolved from a reductionistic perspective on human suffering (abhidharma, higher teaching), to a systems perspective (Madhyamaka/middle-way), and then to a later metasystemic perspective (Buddha-nature) (Guenther, 1989), (Wilber 2014), (D. Brown, personal communication, 2017). Each phase of the teaching is an expression of a cognitive paradigmatic shift in understanding human suffering and happiness and its causes, a turning of the wheel.

THE FIRST TURNING OF THE TEACHING: THE LESSER VEHICLE

The first phase, known as the Hinayana, or Lesser vehicle, due to the focus on individual well-being, was formalized at the third Buddhist council under the patronage of the Indian emperor Ashoka around 250 BCE. It is believed to contain the original teachings of Shakyamuni Buddha (Keown, 2003), and according to Indo-Tibetan hagiography, this first teaching, the first turning of the wheel of dharma, began at Deer Park at the ancient city of Benares (Lopez Jr, 2001). The teaching addresses the cause of existential suffering in the form of dukkha, the suffering of cyclic reactivity, caused by the ordinary mind's conditioned response to mental events. Dukkha is the result of samsara, conditioned reactive cyclic existence, the cycles of repetition compulsion that are caused by ignorance into the nature of awareness and the resulting reactivity that leads to compulsive activity. The great Tibetan meditation master, Kalu Rinpoche, comments on the foundational teachings of cyclic reactivity:

> The small Vehicle is based on becoming aware of the fact that suffering marks all we experience in samsara. Being aware of this engenders the will to rid us of this suffering, to liberate ourselves on an individual level, and to attain happiness. We are moved by our own interest. Renunciation and perseverance allow us to attain our goal. (Kalu Rinpoche (1994, p. 16)

The Buddha approached the analysis of human existential suffering from the perspective of a traditional Ayurvedic medical diagnosis (Bhattacharya, 2003). In this approach are seen the roots of Buddhism as a psychological and therapeutic tradition. The four questions a physician was to ask himself were: 1) is there a disease? If so, what is it? 2) What is the cause of the disease? 3) Is there a cure for the disease? 4) If there is a cure, what is the treatment?

The Buddha's analysis, the four noble truths, began with the observation that there is a human disease, *dukkha*, cyclic reactivity. It does not mean, as early western translations and interpretations would assert, that all life is suffering. The root of the word dukkha is etymologically related in Sanskrit to the prefix *dus* meaning bad, and the word *kha,* the original word for axle hole in the ancient language of the nomadic Aryans. The word dukkha literally means the uncomfortable experience of riding in a wagon when the wheel is off the central axis rather than aligned (Tirch, 2015).

Shakyamuni was pointing to the fact that human life involves some experience of reactivity, traumatic stress, dissatisfaction, and imbalance, no matter how good one has it. Recognizing that the wheel of our life and nervous system is turning off center in a cycle of repetitive stress and trauma is the first step in a process that leads from stressful suffering to wisdom: "The compulsive mind and body, poisoned by narcissistic delusions and destructive emotions, inexorably suffer a life filled with repetitive stress and trauma, preventable illness, premature aging, and meaningless death" (Loizzo, 2015 p. 35). Dukkha is not an esoteric concept, but the Shakya sage's description of the psychology and biology of stress and trauma, which drives each human being to some extent.

The second of the four noble truths is that the cause of dukkha is the mind's conditioning (*karma*) to reactive craving (*tanha*). This addictive grasping of the mind is, according to the Buddhist psychology of information processing (*abhidharma*), driven by the mind's conditioned reactivity to move towards events to create more experience (clinging), to move away from experience to avoid it (aversion), or to lapse into a loss of awareness though fusion with experience (ignorance or confusion). These three compulsive mental activities are said to dominate the normal reactive mind, obscuring the mind's natural condition of openness, clarity, and peace (Brown, 2006). The traditional Buddhist belief is that this cycle of compulsive mental and emotional activity is driven by cause and effect (*karma*) in a multi-life process. Buddhist psychology sees the cycle of psychological reactivity as driven by conditioning inherited from past human and animal lives since *beginingless* time. Reincarnation aside, Shakaymuni's understanding can be interpreted as a naturalistic analysis of suffering describing the conditioning elements of both nature and nurture, the epigenetic transmission of trauma (Yehuda et. al. 2005), "the reincarnation of former ego-structures" (Freud, 1923, p. 48), and the intergenerational transmission of behavior (Loizzo, 2011).

The abhidharma are the systems of Buddhist cognitive psychology that each tradition follows. The Indo-Tibetan tradition draws its abhidharma particularly from the Abhidharmasamuccaya by 4th century Indian Asanga. In the abhidharmic analysis of the causal workings of the mind it reveals that when fully understood there is no solid permanent self but a complex mind-body system of sensations, instincts, emotions, thoughts and perceptual processes known as the five skandhas. When disturbed by traumatic conditioning this system creates the illusion of a permanent self (Tsering, 2010). This sense of a permanent self-existent self is activated due to reactivity caused by cycles of cognitive grasping, aversion and confusion that form a hidden 12-fold cycle, seen below in Figure 1, at the heart of Buddhist psychology. This cycle of traumatic repetition is known as the cycle of dependent origination (*pratityasamutpada*). From the perspective of Buddhist psychology this is the cycle that drives our ordinary unhappiness.

Figure 1
The 12-Link Cycle of Dependent Origination

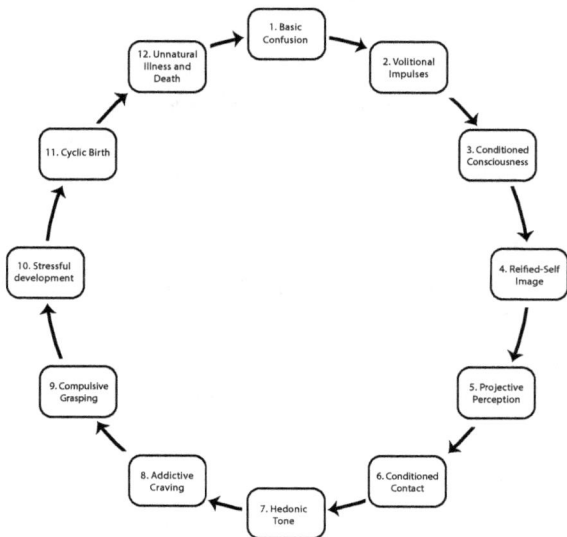

1. Basic Confusion
2. Volitional Impulses
3. Conditioned Consciousness
4. Reified-Self Image
5. Projective Perception
6. Conditioned Contact
7. Hedonic Tone
8. Addictive Craving
9. Compulsive Grasping
10. Stressful development
11. Cyclic Birth
12. Unnatural Illness and Death

Traditionally the cycle is said to operate over three lifetimes (Tashi, 2005). However contemporary Buddhist scholars and psychologists, Batchelor (1998), Loizzo (2011), Miller (2014), and (Neale, 2017) have pointed out these three lifetimes could also refer to one's personal and social past, present and future. Neale (2017) explains that stripping the cycle of its *speculative metaphysics* returns the cycle back to its original intention, which is a psychological model from which psychological karma i.e. causality can be understood. From the discoveries of more contemporary psychology it is understood that humans are deeply conditioned by a childhood past, one that necessarily affects the present, and in turn conditions and creates the future:

> The experiences of the ego seem at first to be lost for inheritance; but when they have been repeated often enough with sufficient strength in many individuals in successive generations, they transform themselves, so to say, into experiences of the id, the impressions of which are preserved by heredity. Thus in the id, which is capable of being inherited, are harbored residues of the existences of countless egos; and, when the ego forms its super-ego out of the id, it may perhaps only be reviving

> shapes of former egos and be bringing them to resurrection. Sigmund Freud. (1990, p. 28)

Animal studies of traumatic prenatal environments have shown that negative influences affect the stress resilience in offspring and result in pathophysiological changes (Kapoor et al., 2004). The growing evidence revealed in animal and human studies shows that stress conditioning extends into future generations, and that the memory of fetal experience extends fetal nutritional and endocrine insults into subsequent generations. The idea presented by the Buddha that prior traumatic conditioning is at the root of the individual's bodymind is now being affirmed by the discoveries of science. Just as research is revealing the epigenetic conditioning of trauma, the opposite is also true, in that the reducing of reactive sensation (link 7) and thus the cutting off of addictive craving (link 8) through mindfulness meditation strengthens mitochondrial function, enhances telomere maintenance, and diminishes expression of inflammatory response genes (Miller, 2014).

Since the 12-link cycle of dependent origination is at the heart of understanding Buddhist psychology it would behoove us to take a deeper look at this cycle and understand it from a contemporary psychological perspective.

1.   **Basic Confusion** (Skt: *avidya*, Tbt: *ma rig-pa*): The mother and father transmit (cause), epigenetically and as part of early childhood socialization, unresolved multi-generational traumatic reactivity (link 13), and the resultant predisposition towards defensive self-protection. This unconscious self-protection leads to the misperception of reality (*avidya*), and the underlying tendency towards reification of the self, others people, and external reality.

2.   **Volitional Impulses** (Skt: *samskara*, Tbt: *'du byed*): This basic confusion of reification (cause) leads to the conditioning of patterns of volitional impulses (*samskara*) that in turn drive emotion and behavior driven through implicit memory. These in turn cause further reactivity and conditioning.

3.   **Conditioned Consciousness** (Skt: *vijnana*, Tbt: *rnamshe*): Through the process of early childhood conditioning in links 1 and 2, the

basic default operating system of consciousness (*vijnana*) is now conditioned by reactive-stress and therefore influencing the processing of sensory and cognitive information and the shaping of all further psychological structures.

4. **Reified-Self Image** (mind and matter) (Skt: *namarupa*, Tbt: *ming gzugs*): This conditioned traumatized consciousness's (link 3) default towards self-protection leads to the creation of an illusory reified self-image built on the building blocks of mind (*nama*) and matter (*rupa*) from the moment-by-moment impermanent flow of the five skandhas or mind/body systems (sensations, feelings, perceptions, mental formations and default consciousness) that form the Buddhist self-system.

5. **Projective Perception** (six sense bases Skt: *ayatana*, Tbt: *phyi'I skye mched drug*): The traumatic self-image (link 4) leads to the distortion of the sense perceptions (link 5) as the biased projection of a threatening world

conditions perception. As such we are no longer seeing the world as it is but through our projective filters. This reinforces our distrust of the world and strengthens defensive reification of the threatened traumatic self-image.

6. **Conditioned Contact** (Sky: *sparsa*, Tbt: *reg pa*) This unconscious traumatic self-image (5) conditions contact (*sparsha*) with the world due to the effect of the distorted self-image and its narrative about the world. This distortion contaminates all experience of life with chronically unsatisfying reactivity.

7. **Hedonic Tone** (Skt: *vedana*, Tbt: *tshor ba*) The conditioning of contact (6) with the world leads to the subjective determinance as to the valence of experiences hedonic tone (*vedana*). This is either pleasant, unpleasant or neutral

8. **Addictive Craving** (Skt: *trsna*, Tbt: *dod sred*): In response to avoid negative hedonic tone, increase pleasurable tone, or ignore

neutral tone (link 7), the bodymind either craves more or less experience. In terms of information processing it either moves away or towards further experience. There are three forms of addictive craving. 1.) The craving of pleasure. 2.) The craving to become, fueled by dissatisfaction with present experience. 3.) The craving for non-existence, which is a response to perceived intolerable experience.

9. **Compulsive Grasping** (Skt: *upadana*, Tbt: *bdag 'dzin*): The addictive craving of experience (link 8) leads to the compulsive grasping (*upadana*) of sense pleasures, and the maintainence of inaccurate worldviews (such as eternalism and nihilism), obsessive behaviors, and identification as a self-existent independent individual.

10. **Stressful development/becoming** (Skt: *bhava*, Tbt: *mi srid*): Compulsive grasping (Link 9) leads to the stressful ongoing development (bhavana) of a self-existent separate self-driven by the misperception of a threatening world.

11. **Cyclic Birth** (Skt: *jati*, Tbt: *skye ba*): The traumatized-self's ongoing development (Link 10) leads to life choices that further condition the self to give birth to traumatic patterns of cyclic repetition (*jati*) that further condition the mind into a life-style of dissatisfaction.

12. **Illness and Death** (Skt: *jaramarana*, Tbt: *rgba 'chi ba*): The effect of giving birth to an unconscious life style (11) leads to an aging and dying process driven by unnatural traumatic stress. This is turn feeds the fear of life, of which aging and death are a natural expression, creating psychological, biological, cultural and systemic dysfunction that becomes the cause for ignorance (1) and the continuation of the cycle of dependent origination.

Buddhist theory and practice is solely designed to end this 12-link process of multigenerational conditioned unhappiness. The understanding of the twelve links is fundamental to understanding how all the different aspects of the Buddhist treatment strategy, the eightfold path, synthesize into an effective path to extinguishing reactive suffering and unfold the human potential for happiness, altruistic activity and evolution.

The third noble truth is that this cycle of reactivity, traumatic repetition and compulsive activity could be ended. Contemporary research into the default mode network of the human brain has revealed that the posterior cingulate cortex implicated in the addictive process of getting caught up in experience is activated similarly in situations of drug addiction, holding to a particular set of beliefs, or self-referential thought processes (Brewer et al., 2013). As such, one can recognize the Buddha's accurate recognition of upadana, the 9th stage of dependent origination, as leading to compulsive grasping of sense pleasures, inaccurate world views, obsessive behaviors and self-referential processing of experience through the faulty view of a self-existent independent individual. The ending of this psychological and biological cycle of reactive grasping, caused by the fundamental confusion of awareness with its conditioned contents (Link 1), is called nirvana, which literally means cessation or extinction. Of note is that extinction is also the term used in behaviorism to refer to the cessation of operant and classically conditioned behavior.

The third truth could equally be called the truth of happiness However, as Loizzo (2012) points out, no positive terms were introduced in fundamental Buddhist psychology of the Hinayana so as not to complicate the formula with a discussion of profound lasting happiness, something that aspirants might find difficult to envision. Therefore, to discuss the third truth in negative terms keeps the formula aligned with its medical/therapeutic intention and to remind us that the cycle of compulsive stress can be permanently extinguished.

The fourth Noble Truth is the Buddhist equivalent of a treatment approach, an eightfold holistic treatment plan of contemplative lifelong healing addressing an accurate view of experience, wholesome intentions, truthful speech, appropriate action, socially beneficial livelihood, consistent effort, and the practices of mindfulness and meditative concentration (Hanh, 1999) (Tsering, 2005). The treatment path (marga) leads to:

1. The development of insight into the three characteristics (impermanence, reactive suffering, and true identity as awareness);

2. The understanding of mental cause and effect as indicated in the cycle of dependent origination, and its relationship to unhappy and happy mental states;

3. The threefold development of ethics, meditative concentration, and psychological insight leading to; and

4. Nirvana, the extinction of the addictive emotional and psychological defilements that cause personal suffering (Loizzo, 2012).

As an integral part of the path, the behavioral interventions of Buddhist ethics are not cast within a simplistic understanding of bad and good, but are understood within the context of the unfolding effects of actions (links 10 and 11) on the strengthening or reducing of the compulsive cycle of dependent origination. In Indo-Tibetan ethics there are 10 inappropriate actions that lead to continuing the cycle of reactive suffering. Violent actions lead to traumatic injury of self and other, compulsive acquisition leads to scarcity consciousness, unnatural sexuality leads to continued sexual frustration, false speech results in mistrust, slander leads to disrepute, abusive speech engenders isolation, idle speech results in contempt, covetous intentions results in mental dissatisfaction, malicious intent results in insecurity, and unrealistic views lead to a confused mind (Loizzo, 2012) On the other hand, the practice of ethically appropriate action creates a very different cycle of cause and effect. Non-violence leads to mental peace, generosity leads to a sense of abundance, sexual sublimation leads to lasting satisfaction, honest speech engenders trust, tactful speech engenders respect, caring speech engenders leadership, meaningful speech engenders authority, philanthropic intent leads to deep contentment, benevolent intent results in confidence, and a realistic view of reality results in clarity of mind (Neale et al., 2017).

The training associated with the turning of the first wheel addresses the problems of personal traumatic conditioning, and, as such, is often referred to as the Hinayana, or personal vehicle, since its focus is the individual rather than the greater community of sentient beings. The ordinary mind of an individual is in a state of constant reactivity to experience through cognitive avoidance (aversion), elaboration of experience (desire) and loss of awareness (confusion/

ignorance). This affects both the mind and the events in the mind in a negative way. From the mind perspective, the reactivity causes mental distractibility, and a discontinuity of awareness. *Mind* here refers to awareness, the basic capability for non-conceptual knowing, and attention, the ability of the mind to hold to a particular mental event. Mental events in Buddhist psychology refer not just to the experience of sensory information (visual, auditory, kinesthetic etc.), but also the processes of thought, memory, and imagination. From the perspective of the mental events, reactivity leads to a disorganization of the unfolding experience in the mind and the constant elaboration of mental content (Brown, 2006).

The goal of treatment/practice is to reduce the causes of reactivity, distractibility, disorganization, and constant mental elaboration, and to increase mental equanimity, the continuity of awareness, the capacity to stay on an intended object-of-focus, to increase organization of mind, and to silence mental activity when needed. The training consists of behavioral modification (ethical precepts), psychoeducation, basic mindfulness and attentional control. Behavioral modifications are designed to interrupt the cycle of dependent origination at the 10th and 11th links by not allowing the development of a lifestyle driven by compulsive grasping and traumatic repetition. Training in the conceptual understanding of the mind (abidharma psychology) helps support an accurate view of the mind and experience to understand the 12 links of dependent origination. Basic mindfulness is practiced to reduce reactivity to unpleasant hedonic experience at the 7th stage. The mindful practice of accepting experience and no longer avoiding unpleasant sensations cuts off the cause for the 8th stage of compulsive grasping. The practice of attentional stability (calm/staying concentration meditation) reconditions the default attentional system at the 3rd stage.

THE SECOND TURNING OF THE TEACHING: THE GREAT VEHICLE

According to the Tibetan tradition, the second phase of the teaching was presented on Vulture Peak Mountain near Rajagriha. It was here that the Buddha was said to have taught on the empty uncompounded nature of all phenomena (Skt: *shunyata*) and on compassion (Skt: *karuna*) (Hanh, 2008). These two elements form the heart of the Mahayana, the Great Vehicle. Historically, the approach is philosophically grounded in the Madhyamaka school founded in the second century CE by Nagarjuna, the abbot of Nalanda University. The Mahayana includes the first turning insights into the reactivity and impermanence of human experience, but deepens the understanding of the deconstruction of the ego (no-self) and impermanence with a more sophisticated understanding that the concepts such as self, suffering, and the freedom from suffering, are themselves empty of an essential nature. In the Mahayana view the entire cycle of dependent origination reviewed earlier is caused by mistaken reification. The fundamental psychological problem with reification (link 1) is that it causes *self grab,*which obscures the natural equanimity of awareness. It is the recognition of the lack of thing-in-itself-ness, the entitylessness, and constructed nature of all phenomena, whether psychological or physical, that is known by the term shunyata, translated as emptiness, but perhaps better served by the term *openness* to ensure that it is not interpreted as a nihilistic vision of human experience when in fact it is the opposite.

In the contemplative approach of the Madhyamaka the mind trained through prior concentration practice (stabilization of link 3) is used to direct a high-speed non-conceptual search through on-going mental experience and the psychological constructions of external reality, to see if any self-existent substantiality can be found (Brown, 1986). This search leads to the experience of the unfindability, unlocatability, and insubstantiality of mental experience, the hallmark of the realization of openness (Hixon, 1993). This is the realization of non-entityness, that the self, its experience, and all external reality are experienced as merely constructs without a substantial self-existent nature (Brown, 2006). "Deep examination of the essence of mind through wisdom will reveal the mind in an ultimate sense to possess neither intrinsic nor extrinsic reality; it is without structure" (Namgyal, p.64).

The stability of attention allows for insight into the process of cyclic traumatic stress, by uncovering the biased self-image at the 4th stage as an impermanent construction, and by disembedding awareness from the contents of experience so that at the 1st link of reified confusion, the cause of afflictive emotions and the entire cycle of suffering starts to be purified of conditioned confused reification. The practice of the insight into the open constructed nature of phenomena (*shunyata*) addresses the reification initiated at the 1st stage and underlying the whole cycle. However, as shall be discussed in Chapter 3, the fundamental reversal of the cycle comes from the permanent transformation of identity by thoroughly cutting the cycle at the first link through the practice of Mahamudra and rDzogchen that directly affirms the clear light nature of awareness as the fundamental open identity of mind.

Following the realization of the emptiness of self and external reality, the contemplative investigation in the second turning of the wheel deepens into examination of the unconscious conditioning of the 1st, 2nd and 3rd links. This is accomplished through the practice of recognizing that time, the temporal unfolding experience of reality, is also a mere construct (Brown, 2006). The realization of this contemplative insight leads to the disembedding of the observing ego from the construct of time, and the experience of a timeless, unchanging awareness. Brown quotes Tashi Namgyal, the author of the Moonlight Mahamudra meditation manual: "the way the realized mind stays (like space) is that there is no elaboration of the three units of time (arising, staying, ceasing, nor any dualities, (eternalism/nihilism, coming/going)" (2006 p. 345). The realization of the mind's timelessness opens the meditator to the experience of the simultaneous interconnectedness of all potential events. This realization in the Mahayana is what matures into the realization of compassion and the importance of the transformation of society, as all beings are intimately and simultaneously interconnected.

THE THIRD TURNING OF THE TEACHING:
THE BUDDHA-NATURE VEHICLE

*I*t is believed in the Tibetan tradition that the third turning was taught by the historical Buddha to an audience of Bodhisattvas at a number of locations in India. Historically, the philosophical foundations are found in the yogachara school, originating in the fourth century with Asanga guided by his visionary experiences of Maitreya, the mythic Buddha of the future. Whilst the Madhyamaka school asserts the fundamental unconstructed nature of human experience, the yogachara school asserts that the mind, awareness, has a primordial reality, and that this mind essence, or Buddha-nature (Skt: *tathagatagarbha*) is ultimately real. Later Indian masters from Nalanda University integrated the Madhyamaka and the yogachara view into the *yogacara-svatantrika-Madhyamaka*. This position held the Madhyamaka position that reality is essentially empty but that the methodology of the yogachara school helped students progress along the path to that realization (Mipham, 2005). Whilst the Indo-Tibetan tradition has multiple lineages with slightly differing approaches, in essence they address the same issue.

From the point of view of individually ascribed names, there are numerous traditions, such as those of the simultaneously arising as merged, the amulet box, possessing five, the six spheres of equal taste, the four syllables, the pacifier, the object to be cut off, rDzogchen, the discursive Madhyamaka view, and so on. Nevertheless, when scrutinized by a yogi, learned in scripture and logic and experienced (in meditation), their definitive meanings are all seen to come to the same intended point. (The First Panchen Lama, Lozang-chokyi-gyeltsen, (Berzin translator), 1997, p.98).

The yogachara terminology is used by the Tibetan essence of mind traditions to explain their most refined practices, the generation and completion stage (*tantra*), great seal, (Skt: *mahamudra*) and great completion (Tbt: *rdzog chen*) traditions. Whilst the three approaches of tantra, Mahamudra, and rDzogchen have differing terminology and methodology in realizing the Buddha-nature, they generally agree that the fundamental basis of awareness is a non-dual union of openness/spaciousness/mother consciousness and the clear-light awareness/lucid knowing/infant consciousness, the union of which is also known as the dharmakaya, the body of truth. It is the recognition of this fundamental awareness at the 1st link that cuts the entire traumatic repetition of dependent origination.

The mother, openness, is the phenomenological open basis, ground, and foundation of all experience. The Bon rDzogchen lineage of Zhan Zhung Nyan Gyud, describes it as the *space of the nature of phenomena* with nine qualities: boundlessness, omnipervasiveness, and unlimited expansiveness, without top or bottom, immeasurableness, uncontractedness, great vastness, everlasting and immutable (Wangyal, 2000). This open phenomenological space is described as *the Mother* because it is the mother of all phenomenological existence, freedom and conditionality, matter and mind, good and bad, truth and illusion. Thus, this openness is not an inert void, "is not some abstracted and lifeless emptiness, but an utter fullness that.... is vibrant with energy" (Guenther, 1989 p. 203). In a similar way the open field of outer space is full of the fecundity of galaxies, stars, and solar systems. It is not an abstract void-instead a field full of life.

On the other hand, the infant consciousness is the primordial, lucid nature of the mind, an awareness that is brilliantly awake, referenceless, pristinely non-conceptual, and the most basic form of cognition or knowing. At the deepest fundamental levels of the human mind the unbounded openness is inseparable from this referenceless clear knowing.

In the Indo-Tibetan tradition the first turning of the wheel focuses on treating traumatic reactivity and suffering through understanding the cycle of dependent origination that conditions experience, the ethical practice of behavioral modification (links 9,10,11), mindfulness meditation (link 7), and the attentional development of calm/staying (link 3). In the second turning treatment focus is on practicing recognizing the fundamental openness of experience to liberate the mind from the human habit to reify all experience of self, other, and the world. This matures into the understanding that the entire cyclic nature of suffering is caused by the failure to recognize openness and the ensuing reactive reification. In the third turning of wheel it is understood that suffering is due to basic confusion and ignorance, (Skt: *avidya*, Tbt: *marigpa*) as to the true nature of the buddha mind that is always already right here (link 1). The recognition of the Buddha-nature is obscured by the ordinary operations of consciousness, including even the activity of meditation itself. The aim of treatment of this cognitive dis-ease in the Mahamudra and rDzogchen traditions is of a similar nature, but the methods differ slightly.

CHAPTER THREE

BUDDHIST ESSENCE PSYCHOLOGY

*A*s mentioned in chapter two the Buddhist tradition of contemplative psychology can be divided into three developmental stages (lesser, greater, and buddha/essence vehicles). This stage progression of understanding and treating the causes of cyclic reactive suffering (*dukkha*) transcend and include each prior stage. This chapter investigates the contemplative psychology of the third paradigm, the essence traditions of Mahamudra and rDzogchen, and how these teachings have their foundation in the fundamental insights of the first and second turnings, but also expands upon them by exploring the nature of mind: the clear light spacious nature of awareness itself. It is this essence tradition of contemplative psychology that is the focus of this exploration.

Within the Indo-Tibetan tradition there arose in the 19th century, in response to the authoritarianism of the ruling Gelugpa order, an ecumenical movement known as the rime (all-embracing, unlimited, impartial (Schaik, 2011). This universal approach to contemplative practice respected the separate lineages and yet was able to draw upon the best elements of the five schools. This movement continues today and is best personified in His Holiness the 14th Dalai Lama, who studied with many great masters across the tradition, and took His Holiness Menri Trizin, the leader of the indigenous Bon tradition, as one of his mentors in rDzogchen (great completion) practice.

An outcome of this non-sectarian movement was the synthesis of the Mahamudra and rDzogchen traditions. Meditation masters such as the 3rd Karmapa, 5th, 13th and the 14th Dalai Lama worked with both Mahamudra and rDzogchen practice. An excellent example of this movement is the text *Buddhahood in the Palm of the Hand, The Union of Mahamudra and rDzogchen* by the 17th century master karma chags-med (Chagme, 2000). The text outlines a path of practice using Mahamudra to recognize and stabilize the realization of Buddha-nature, and then the use of rDzogchen practice to bring that realization to fruition. Rime masters tend to use Mahamudra first, as it best outlines the path of awakening to the buddha mind, and then rDzogchen that has a clear outline as to the completion of the path, buddhahood (Rinpoche, 1989).

MAHAMUDRA

*M*ahamudra (*phyag chen*), the *great seal, great embrace*, or *great symbol* is a tradition of concepts and practices within the Indo-Tibetan Buddhist tradition. Maha means great in the sense of a great openness beyond limitations, and mudra refers to the expressive nature of phenomenal experience as viewed from the awakened mind (Ray, 2002).

Mahamudra is divided into sutra, tantra, and essence approaches. Sutra Mahamudra is based on the Buddha-nature teachings of the third turning of the uttaratantra shastra of Maitreya (Gyamtso, 2000) and outlines a path to realization attained through the practice of the six paramitas as the bodhisattva aspirant journeys five paths and ten stages to buddhahood). Tantra Mahamudra is based on the anuttarayoga tantras (unsurpassable union process) of the New Translation school and outlines a path of practice based on the transformation of the self-image, inner narrative, neurochemistry and energy system of the individual through visualization and yogic exercise (Loizzo, 2012). Essence Mahamudra refers to the approach of direct investigation into the nature of mind and it is comparable to the rDzogchen teachings of the rNing ma and Bon traditions (Ringu, 2007).

> There is the scholastic Mahayana path of the perfections (*paramitayana*), which takes inference for its path. There is the Mahayana path of mantra (*mantrayana*), which takes the guru's sustaining spiritual power for its path based on the stages of generation and completion. There is the innate and spontaneously arising luminous mind of the Great Seal (*mahamudra*) that takes direct perception (skt: *pratyaksa*) for its path. (SGam po pa, 2012, p.53)

The essence tradition of Mahamudra originates with the great adept Saraha, who it is believed lived in India in the first millennium CE. He is regarded by the Tibetan tradition to have been the teacher of the philosopher and abbot of Nalanda monastery, Nagarjuna, and the mountain hermit Savaripa. Maitripa (986-1063), received visionary instruction from Savaripa, and outlined in his written works the doctrine of 'not taking to mind' (amanisakara), mentioned below.

In Tibet there are numerable lineages of Mahamudra practice in the Kagyu, Sakya and Gelug traditions of the new translation school. Important to the lineage of Mahamudra practice described in this chapter is the Tibetan translator, Mar pa Chos kyi bLo gros (1012-97) who studied essence Mahamudra with Maitripa, and tantra Mahamudra with the ex-abbot of Nalanda, Naropa (d. 1040). Mar pa brought the Mahamudra teachings to Tibet and transmitted them to a number of students the most renowned being rJe btsun mi la ras pa (1052-1135). Mi la ras pa passed these teachings to his disciples the yogi Ras chung rdo rdo rje grags pa (1083-1161), and the monastic physician sGam po pa (1079-1153). It is the physician sGam po pa who founded Dagpo bka' brgyud Monastery and initiated the bka'brgyud monastic lineage that continues to this day under the direction of the 17th Karmapa. sGam po pa, taking his lead from the sutra Mahamudra teachings in Maitreya's uttaratantra, decided to teach a number of students the essence approach to understanding the nature of mind within an unorthodox graduated curriculum of practice without requiring the extensive rituals and practices of the tantric approach (Jackson, 2011) (Ray, 2002) (Brown, 2006).

This new approach to Mahamudra outlined in sGam po pa's *Explanation of the Sole Path of Mahamudra* outlines the practices in a four yoga model comprising preliminary practices to prepare the mind and body, ordinary calm/staying practice to calm the events of the mind and develop attentional stability, ordinary special insight practices to recognize the empty lucid nature of awareness, and the extraordinary practices to recognize the non-duality of appearance/awareness-emptiness, and to effortlessly mature the realization (Brown, 2006).

> A lucid, unceasing momentary awareness is the one-pointed stage of yoga. Understanding the essential nature of that awareness as nonarising emptiness that transcends conceptual modes or reality and unreality is the nondiscriminatory yoga. Understanding diverse appearances as being one from the standpoint of their intrinsic nature is the one-taste yoga. An unceasing realization of the union of appearance and its intrinsic emptiness is the great equipoise of nonmeditation yoga. (sGam po pa in Namgyal, 1986 p. 358)

The four yogas are also known by the names of Shamatha, Vipashyana, Yugganaddha, and Mahamudra. As rDzogchen Ponlop Rinpoche, a contemporary master of the and rNing ma lineages puts it:

> One begins with the practice of shamatha; on the basis of that, it becomes possible to practice vipashyana or lhagthong. Through one's practice of vipashyana being based on and carried on in the midst of shamatha, one eventually ends up practicing a unification [yuganaddha] of shamatha and vipashyana. The unification leads to a very clear and direct experience of the nature of all things. This brings one very close to what is called the absolute truth Mahamudra. (Ray, 2004, p.76)

THE PATH OF DEVELOPMENT
IN MAHAMUDRA

*I*n order to understand Mahamudra it is necessary to understand the concept of *tawa (Tbt.)* or *dristi (Skt.)* which literally means, *view,* meaning the view from which one experiences phenomena. Brown (2017) explains that the view is dependent upon the basis of mental operation (*spod yu*), the loci of identity, level of awareness or vantage point from where the mind's metacognition is operating. According to Ras chung, student of Mi la ras pa, there are four main bases of operation, see Table 1 below (awareness fused with thought and self-structure, awareness beyond self-structure, awareness beyond temporal processing, and awareness beyond the information processing system), with each level sequentially freer from the subtler and subtler reifications of unconscious psychological and perceptual structures. Each basis of operation has the capacity to view phenomena (take the event perspective) and self-recognition (the mind perspective). The event perspective refers to the perspective of mental objects perceived at that particular level of awareness i.e. concrete objects such as the thoughts and subtle objects such as abstract patterns. The mind perspective refers to the perspectival capacity to self-reflect and recognize the level of awareness from which the mind is operating i.e. to make awareness, the subject, the object of itself.

Indo-Tibetan psychology is based on an understanding of four levels of mind; the coarse, subtle, very subtle and awakened. These are four levels of mental experience are are always present in experience, but they are not necessary conscious. Whether a level of mind is made conscious or not is dependent on the level of view, the basis of operation from which identity is operating. Therefore, the basis of operation moves through the various levels of mind. The course level of mind is the level of day-to-day experience based in the linguistically created world of thought by the self. At this level of mind, the events we perceive are solid, a reified world of objects based on language. The next level of mind is the subtle level of mind that is perceived in information processing prior to naming of the coarse level. At this level the events are just the high-speed movement of perceptual information such as the abstract patterning of pure sensation, sound, and color. The mind at this level is functioning prior to thought, and the construction of self, and if the basis of operation is operating at this level it functions beyond the structure of self. The third level of mind is the very subtle level of mind. At this level the mind is a vast interconnected spacious field of very subtle energy and the basis of operation that perceives this is level of mind is a timeless, non-dual individual basis of operation. The fourth level of mind referred to earlier as the Buddha-nature, Dharmakaya, is a non-dual unity of referenceless awareness (*rigpa*) and unbounded space (*ma*) where the field and the basis of operation perceiving the field are undivided. These four levels of mind and their perceived objects are shown below in Table 1.

Table 1

Levels of Mind, Basis of Operation & Event

Level of Mind	Basis of operation	Event Perspectives
Coarse	Awareness fused with thought and self-structure	Solid object
Subtle	Awareness beyond self-structure	Energetic object
Very Subtle	Awareness beyond temporal processing	Interconnected field
Awakened	Awareness beyond information processing	Space

The table above shows a basic relationship between the level of mind, the event experienced at that level of mind, and the basis of identity operation at that particular level. The basis of operation shifts during meditation and initially this will be a brief *state* but as practice continues the state will become a *trait*, and a permanent developmental stage of identity. The levels of mind, basis of operation, and objects are also hierarchically nested, which means that when operating from awakened awareness beyond information processing that the awareness can cognize space, the interconnected field, energetic objects and solid objects. However, when awareness is fused with thought and self-structure it will be unable to perceive the subtle, very subtle levels of mind.

Next, we are going to examine the four-yoga model of sGam po pa's Mahamudra to see how the practice unfolds through the developmental sequence of disembedding awareness as basis of operation from subtler and subtler psychological structures.

sGam po pa's Four-Yoga Model

sGam po pa's four-yoga model meditation practice is designed to facilitate shifting from one basis of operation to another The meditator first calms the mind (*shamatha*), then by gaining insight (*vipashyana*) into the constructed nature of the self, time, and individuality recognizes awareness to be already beyond all structures to a basis of operation, Buddha-nature, without any reference points (Brown, 2006).

One-pointed yoga: calm/staying (shamatha). The practice of calm/staying refers to the calming of mental events in the mind such as thought and conflicting emotions, and the staying of the attentional system on the chosen object of mediation. The basic cognitive skills to be developed are motivation, directing attention, intensifying the attentional interest to the object, and metacognitive awareness.

Motivation needs to be developed to get the practitioner to begin and continue the process of practice. Steering involves the repeated redirection of the wandered attention back to the meditation object. It would be akin to placing and replacing a slide under a microscope. The student learns to intensify the attention by increasing the interest in the meditation object. The practitioner learns to have volitional access of the attention, developing the capacity to shift from vague interest to admiration to fascination of the object by increasing the salience of the details presented whether that is the breath, sensations of the body, a visual object, thought (*mantra*), or visualization. This would be akin to zooming in to have a close look at an object under the microscope.

Metacognition in the context of calm/staying meditation is related to the non-conceptual intelligence, or clarity of knowing what is arising within the experience of the meditator, and therefore being able to adjust the meditation accordingly. Metacognition is the bright light that illuminates the slide in one's contemplative microscope metaphor, and allows one to have a close and clear look at the slide.

As students learn to develop calm staying, they sequentially work through the ability to steer, intensify the attention, and brighten metacognition. The tradition has a number of ways of breaking up the stages of calm/staying but essentially the meditation has two main phases: with support, and without support. Calm staying with support describes the development of continuous and complete staying on the meditation object where the object still appears to be permanent and therefore the mind is operating at the coarse level of operations. Calming staying without support refers to the development of the capacity to stay so close to the object that the meditator becomes aware of the impermanent nature of the meditation object as momentary perceptual pixels of information.

Non-discriminatory yoga: insight (vipashyana). Once the meditator develops the capacity for calm/ staying he or she is ready to use the stable mind to gain insight into the constructed nature (emptiness) of psychological reality. The function of insight meditation is twofold. First, to come to understand that all psychological phenomena that arise in experience (perceptual, cognitive, affective, and physical) are psychologically constructed. This first stage of the practice is a negation of the thing-in-itself-ness of the object. It leads to an experience of the psychological openness of experience that releases the 'grab" of the object over the attentional system, which in turn allows for the second stage, which is a clear recognition of the nature of the awareness that perceives the object.

The insight practice typically focuses on first coming to understand the entitylessness of the self. According to the Mahayana tradition it is the *grasping onto self* that is the root of all ignorance (Lamrimpa, 2002). Ignorance can also be translated as *confusion*, i.e. the fusion of awareness with the self that is the root of all confusion. The realization of the emptiness of self happens through a meditative search into the meditator's direct experience to see if the self can be discovered as a substantial independent entity. This culminates in the direct experience of the nonentityness of the self, the experience of emptiness. The realization of the emptiness of experience can then be generalized to all other psychological structures and experience such as thought, the body, emotional states, pain, etc.

> When the mind is viewed from the perspective of the observer, no inherent self-existing, self-representation can be found. This is emptiness of the person. When the mind is viewed from the event-perspective the events are found neither to be solid, inherently self-existent, nor durable. This is the emptiness of phenomena. Brown (2006, p. 287)

Brown (2006) in his synthetic review of Mahamudra through the structure of the four yogas breaks the phases of special insight into the emptiness of self, phenomena, and time. This last stage, the emptiness of time, sets up the basis of psychological operation needed at the beginning of the yoga of One Taste. Awareness of the emptiness of time deepens the contemplative analysis of experience via insight in meditation that the deepest substrate of awareness does not arise and pass away like temporal experience, but functions outside the construct of past, present, and future and is continuously operating even during waking, dreaming and deep sleep states (Mason, 2010). This is the realization of the very subtle level of mind that is the psychological basis of operations of all the further Mahamudra meditations.

One taste yoga: union of calm staying & insight.
The basis of psychological operation for the one taste yoga (*yugganaddha*) is the very subtle, timeless level of awareness. This basis of operation is established by investigating that awareness itself is changeless and beyond the conventional coming and going of time. Exploring the timelessness of the spacious phenomenological field of perception, and then recognizing the nature of the awareness that perceives such field can also establish timeless awareness.

Tashi Namgyal explains that there are three things to be determined about the abiding nature of this very subtle mind, its essence, nature, and characteristics. The essence of mind is empty, self-nature is luminous clarity, and its aspects consist of the diverse display of experience appearance.

The practitioner recognizes that this field of non-conceptual awareness and phenomenological space is inseparable and extends in all directions without boundary. Again quoting Namgyal (p. 216), "Whatever is the nature of space is the nature of awareness. Whatever is the nature of awareness is enlightenment. For this reason awareness, the expanse of space and the mind of enlightenment, are nondual and inseparable"

This is called *establishing the view*. In essence practice the meditations are less about meditating on something as they are about learning to operate from a new level of awareness, a new basis of operation, and from there to take a new perspective or view on experience. The prior calm/staying training is needed for the stability and capacity to hold the perspective long enough for it to become established.

Once the view of the empty lucid nature of the very subtle level of mind is stable the practitioner learns *reverse samadhi*, to ease up on the relative activity of ordinary coarse level thinking, but to simultaneously maintain the view. Then whatever mental events arise moment-by-moment within the field of the very subtle level of mind is experienced as the non-dual expression of this field. Non-dual here means that the unbounded field of awareness-space and the objects in awareness arise together, and are *co-emergent* (Namgyal) and *simultaneously* (Brown, 2005) arising.

'When the meditator perceives the clarity of perceptive form and its unidentifiable emptiness as being the inseparable, denuded union of appearance and emptiness or emptiness and appearance, he has gained insight into the intrinsic coemergence of appearance" (Namgyal, p. 233). Tashi Namgyal (p. 225) lays out three stages to the actual identification of the spontaneous coemergence: identifying the mind co-emergence of the mind, which addresses the mind perspective, and the cognitive co-emergence of mental activity and perceptual appearance, which address the event perspective. Brown (2005) calls these mind-simultaneous, cognition-simultaneous, and appearance-simultaneous.

The meditation on the simultaneous co-emergent mind is a process of deeper and deeper familiarization with the inseparability and one taste of the empty lucid awareness and the manifestations of appearance. Initially the student realizes the inseparable nondual nature of the simultaneous co-emergent mind with all cognition and appearance. As the meditation deepens the reactive identification with objects releases and then finally as it matures there is no distinction between awareness and its content. Namgyal refers to this realization as recognizing the abiding nature of awareness as identical with the ordinary mind (p.244). Where ordinary refers to the naturalness of the mind rather than its mundanity.

Non-meditation yoga (Mahamudra). At the heart of the Mahamudra approach to addressing basic confusion, and associated with adepts Saraha, Maitripa, and Tilopa is the doctrine and practice of amanisakara. Amanisakara (Tibetan: *Yi la mi byed pa*) is translated as *non-mentation*, *non-egocentricity*, *not taking to mind*, and *non-particularization*. It is at the heart of the third turning approach to contemplative practice (Higgins, 2006) (Brown, 2006).

In the psychology of the abhidharma, the manisakara is the last in a sequence of five omnipresent mental factors of information processing (contact, discernment, feeling, intention and attention) (Tashi, 2010) that are active in every moment of experience. Manisakara has numerous translations, *attention* (Tashi,) *ego centric demanding* (Guenther & Kawamura, 1975), *bringing to mind*, *setting one's mind upon*, *focus* (Higgins, 2006) *taking to mind, mental engagement, particularizing* (Brown, 2006), *paying attention*, or *taking to mind* (Berzin, 2017). Essentially, manisakara is the activity of the information processing system that engages with a mental event and in doing so simultaneously creates the experience of subject and object, the attention and the attended. If awareness is confused with this attentional movement, it then identifies itself solely as the attentional system and then the larger field of open phenomenological experience (Ground) will be obscured. The construction of an object simultaneously obscures the larger phenomenological field of space, just as awareness's fusion with the attentional subject obscures the pristine open cognition of the infant consciousness. Brown (2006 p. 438) refers to this attentional subject as *individual consciousness*.

Amanisakara is the non-meditation discipline that follows the prior three yogas and provides the meditator with the conditions to realize the nature of mind. In the term *amanisakara* the beginning *A* is a negative particle, and is referring to the negation of the information processing and attentional system (manisakara) of individual consciousness. This is achieved through orienting the nondual timeless awareness beyond identification with the artificial mental engagement of information processing, and towards any specific object towards the whole field of experience. Nonmeditation (*sgom med*) means precisely this: doing away with any artificial activity that can be considered meditation" (Brown, 2006 p 412).

> When the mind does not move toward any seeming appearing object, and more specifically does-not-take-it to-mind, the

most rudimentary basis for any discrimination falls away, and the practitioner completely transcends all false conceptualization. Mastery of not-taking-to-mind completely purifies the mind of any tendency to move toward or away from seeming objects. Specifically, it eradicates any movement of the mind-perceiver and clears the way for undistracted awareness of the natural mind. Brown (2006, p. 415)

By perfecting this non-meditation, the meditator attains naked, unsupported awareness. This nondiscriminatory awareness is the meditation! By transcending the duality of meditation and meditator, external and internal realities, the meditating awareness dissolves itself into its luminous clarity. Transcending the intellect is without the duality of equipoise and post-equipoise. Such is the quintessence of mind. Je Phadru (Namgyal, p. 361)

MAHAMUDRA AND BRAIN RESEARCH

Drs. Brown, Brewer, Schoenberg, and this author recently completed a study with 30 intermediate level meditators that elucidated these stages of Mahamudra meditation as having clear and distinct neurological signatures common to meditators at each stage of meditation (Schoenberg, et. al., 2018).

The study gave the first neurophysiological correlates of discrete mental states during Indo-Tibetan essence-of-mind practice using electroencephalography (EEG). The empirical approach targeted time-frequency-spatial information within the EEG signal using Low Resolution Electromagnetic Tomography Analysis (LORETA) to discrete alpha, beta, and gamma bandwidths. The contribution of this study was its focus on the process of awakening as discussed in this chapter. The two higher stages of Mahamudra meditation, one-taste yoga and non-meditation yoga were differentiated into four specific meditative stages with each yoga comprising two meditative states.

The EEG findings indicated two major patterns. The first was that the current density upon entering the meditation state weakened in comparison to baseline control conditions observed in all frequencies and regions of interest. It is hypothesized that this was because the foundation of essence of mind meditation practice is to shift out of the cognitive/brain effort-effortless axis into recognizing aspects of mental experience that are always already present.

The second main finding was that while the default mode network activity in the medial ventral pre-frontal cortex and posterior cingulate cortex did not significantly increase across meditative states there was a unification of enhanced beta and gamma band density magnitude increasing from meditation state 1 (ocean and waves) through to meditation state 4 (stabilized non-meditation awakened awareness) that spanned the anterior cingulate cortex (ACC), precuneus, and parietal lobes.

This separation of the default-mode network and the executive functioning system reveals an active executive functioning and yet non-self-referential pattern of activity i.e. the executive functioning of the brain was operational while the basis of operation shifted beyond the self-structure to timeless awareness and then awakened awareness.

The results also indicate that as progression of the effortlessness became stronger there was enhanced ACC (executive functioning/self-regulation), parietal and insular activation suggesting the activation of brain networks associate with saliency, conflict monitoring, emotional control and shifts in perspective-taking that are inferred as supporting the very subtle meditative states of spacious awareness, non-duality, emptiness of phenomena, lucidity and referencelessness.

Numerous EEG studies have revealed that EEG

bands in the higher frequencies (beta, gamma) have been associated with the experiences of selflessness, non-judgmental awareness, and compassionate loving kindness (Schoenberg et.al, 2017). The Indo-Tibetan essence-of-mind research showed that the anterior cingulate cortex (ACC), the central brain structure involved in executive functioning, (working memory, theory of mind tasks, encoding reward prediction and prediction error, emotional regulation, cognitive processing), homeostatic physical states (hunger, thirst, awareness of breath etc.), and the encoding of stimuli valence through sensory modalities was active in the gamma bandwidth. This suggests enhanced activity of executive control capacities increasingly engage in maintaining *the view* as the practitioners shifted to deeper level of natural effortless meditation.

Increases in Gamma frequencies were also recorded in the parietal pathways of which the ventral stream relates to perspective shifting, such as from a first person subjective perspective to that of a third person observer. Simultaneous to the continued activation of the parietal pathways, the self-referencing activity associated with the posterior cingulate cortex (PCC), part of the default mode network, remained deactivated throughout the stages of meditation. This was interpreted as relating to the phenomenological shifting from identification with the self (PCC) and to that of a referenceless basis of operation (parietal).

Beta frequency in the insular cortex associated with the metacognitive awareness and the modulation of interoceptive and emotional stimuli were also recorded. The researchers hypothesized that this was a possible neural marker for the non-preference or *equanimity* towards internal stimuli, which is a central marker of stage four, awakened awareness.

Further research is warranted, but one might hypothesize from the results that just as these states give specific neurological signatures so will the trait acquisition of these states as a permanent basis of psychological operation show specific neurological signatures. As practitioners engage in repeated meditative state practice, and the integration of the state into their lives, their basis of operation begins to permanently shift, and this is paralleled by a transformation in the neurological activity of the brain that can be measured. It is hoped that such research will support the legitimization of Indo-Tibetan contemplative psychology as a powerful means of reducing suffering and supporting the flourishing of positive mental states and altruistic engagement.

rDZOGCHEN

rDzogchen, or great completion practice, is the culmination of contemplative practice in the indigenous Bon tradition and the oldest Buddhist tradition in Tibet, the rNing ma. In both systems it is the apex of nine stages where each system is a practice path unto itself, and there are different paths of practice for different levels of understanding. In the Bon tradition the lower stages focus on shamanic practice while the rNing ma model addresses the foundational Buddhist practices of the Hinayana. Both traditions then progress through Bodhisattva teachings on emptiness and compassion, and then Tantric approaches using visualization and yogic techniques to culminate in rDzogchen.

CLASSIFICATIONS OF rDZOGCHEN

rNing ma schools have classified the rDzogchen teaching into three series of teachings. The first is the *sems sde*, or *mind series*, which provides the most detailed step-by-step explanation and instruction in the path with an emphasis on non-conceptual awareness knowing. This approach is similar to the four yoga model of sGam po pa. The second series is the *klong de*, or *space series*, where the approach is more direct, immediate and emphasizes non-conceptual space. The methods rely upon remaining within the meditative view through the use of sensation and other direct sensory experience. Particular postures, belts, and sticks are used as a support to create powerful sensory experience through which the practitioner can easily recognize directly the phenomenological unbounded openness of experience (Chogyam, 2002). The third series is the *mengak de, the secret precept series*, which contains little instruction, just simple descriptions and methods on how to maintain the view. The late Dudjom Rinpoche, leader of the rNing ma school clarified that the Mind series attracts those attached to mind, the Space series attracts those individual predisposed to spaciness, and the Secret Precept series appeals to those with aversion to a graduated path (Keith Dowman, 2017).

As an example of the rDzogchen tradition this exploration will focus on the A Khrid system from Bon rDzogchen. The A Khrid tradition with its clear step-by-step systematized and manualized approach to contemplative practice is akin to the popular treatment manuals in contemporary psychotherapy. As a system it could be classified as a mind series of instructions within the rNing ma system and the comparable to the approach of sGam po pa's Mahamudra (Reynolds, 2014). As such it provides a systemized approach that parallels and expands upon the Mahamudra four-yoga model.

Bon is the indigenous tradition of the Tibetan plateau that originated from an ancient empire, Zhang Zhung, that includes areas known today as Iran, Tajikistan Afghanistan, Tibet, Kashmir, Pakistan, and India (Reynolds, 2014, & Brown, 2017). The founder of the tradition was a Buddha known as sTon pa gShen rab who predated the Indian Shakyamuni Buddha by many centuries. According to the Bon tradition itself sTon pa gShen rab is recorded as having lived approximately 9800 years ago (Martin, 2009). The Shen clan continues today as one of the main Bonpo family lineages.

The Bon tradition is composed of both shamanic ritual practices for gaining benefit and prosperity in this life known as the causal Bon (*rgyu'i bon*), and those higher spiritual teachings of Tönpa Sherab, known as the fruitional Bon (*'bras bu'i bon*) which consist of sutra, tantra and rDzogchen practices akin to those found in the Buddhist lineages originating from India (Reynolds, 2014, & Brown, 2017).

There are four transmission lineages of rDzogchen within Bon; the Zhang-zhung snyan rgyud (Oral transmission from Zhang Zhung), the rDzog chen yang rtse klong chen (The Great Perfection from the Highest Peak of the Great Vast Expanse), the Ye khri mtha sel (Removing Limitations from the Primordial State) and the A Khrid (the Guiding Explanation for the Primordial State) (Reynolds, 2005). The A Khrid system of meditation was mainly practiced at Menri monastery, the seat of the tradition. The lineage originates from rMe'u ston dGongs mdzod Ri khrod Chenpo (1038-1096), who synthesized prior cycles of teachings into an 80-session course of contemplative study (Achard, 2012) (Reynolds, 2005). After Ri khro, 'the Great Hermit', the A Khrid manual of practice was transmitted through nine generations and in the process was condensed to 30 sessions. The ninth lineage folder of the A Khrid system Bru rGyal ba g.Yung drung (1242-1290) condensed the system to a 15 session manual which became the most popular version of the A Khrid teachings, and the one discussed below. The A Khrid teachings were brought to the West after the master sLod dpon Sangs rgyas bsTan 'dzin (d.1977) received a vision from the Bon protective deity, Ma mchog Srid pa'igyalmo, in which he was informed that to preserve the Bon tradition the teachings would need to be written down and taught across the world, including the West (Brown, 2017).

The A Khrid System of rDzogchen

*B*rown & Gurung (2017) in their translation of the A Khrid pith instructions reveal how the commentary of the A Khrid divides practice into three main phases: bringing the unripened mind stream to ripening, bringing the ripened mind stream to liberation, and bringing the liberated mind-stream to the completion of Buddhahood.

Ripening the unripened mind stream. The unripened mind is brought to ripening through four sessions of practice. These sessions of practice can vary in length depending on the capacity of the practitioner. Whether the session takes days, weeks, or months, the session is completed when the practitioner's meditation shows the relevant signs of maturation as indicated by the text and commentaries. The first *Meditation on Impermanence* weakens the practitioner's attachment to everyday affairs and increases the desire for contemplative development.

> Years keep blending into months. Months keep blending into days. The exact time of reaching death cannot be planned. The exact time of death is uncertain. The conditions of death are uncertain. The only thing that remains is that you will die. Then you will not hold onto anything or any other person whatsoever. Your time of death is unpredictable. Druchen Gyalwa Yungdrung. (2017, p. 57)

By reminding the practitioner of the precious opportunity presented by access to the teachings, and the impermanence of life with no clear knowledge of when their death might occur, the motivation of the student is increased to a level of peak performance necessary to make developmental gains.

The second session, *Setting the Intention and Taking Refuge*, is designed to set a strong motivation directed by a compassionate intention to serve all beings, and develop a deep bond of trust and faith in the masters of the lineage and their positive influence on the contemplative practice.

The third session, the *Mandala Offering*, is a symbolic act of making offerings. This is designed to increase the ratio of positive mental states to negative states of mind, and therefore support the cultivation of wisdom and compassion. Through visualization the practitioner builds an imaginal representation of great human and natural riches; beautiful mansions, jewels, works of art, gardens, forests, oceans etc. The practitioner generates visual, auditory, olfactory and gustatory representations and then practices offering this virtual universe and all its inhabitants to the teacher and the lineage. Since the mind and brain responds to imagery with the same conditioning as actual sensory experience the repeated acts of generosity loosen selfishness. In Buddhist psychology it is understood that generosity makes the mind more open and spacious reducing the cognitive and affective agitation caused by self-grasping.

The fourth session is the *Guru Yoga*, or *mentor bonding* practice, through which the meditators open themselves to the *influence of the gift waves* by internalizing their mentor through the practice of visualization. It is through this process that the seed of the practice that will bear fruit as Buddhahood is both internalized as the inner master, and recognized as the essence of the meditator's own mind.

Bringing the Ripened Mind-Stream to Liberation. The ripened mind is brought to liberation through the second phase of six sessions. These sessions traverse the same psychological territory as the four yogas of Mahamudra. Session five and six, *Concentration With and Without Attributes,* are devoted to calming the events of the mind and developing attentional stability. First by using a meditation object, in this case a Tibetan letter *A*, and then secondly by resting the mind directly into the awake, empty, rootless, relaxed and still nature of awareness.

Through the seventh session, *Bringing Forth the Benefit,* the practitioner recognizes his or her basis of identity and psychological operation as being beyond the constructions of self, and time. Through the practice of mixing awareness into the visual perception of the outer open sky itself, and recognizing the perceptual non-duality between the awareness that is seeing the sky and the openness of the cloudless sky, one come's to recognize the spacious field of lucid, intense, and brilliantly awake awareness that is always present in each moment.

Directed at the clear sky, free of clouds of wind, set up the essential body points and gaze as previously described, and let the [view arise

Focus your awareness on the surrounding space. Mix together the [surrounding] space and awareness completely [until it is one field of empty awareness-space]. Suddenly they will come together. Druchen Gyalwa Yungdrung. (2017, p. 117)

The eighth session, *Pointing Out the Meaning of the Natural State*, relies upon the practice of breath retention (vase breathing) and meditation on the central channel. This approach uses the altered state produced to eradicate the mind's coarse layer of conceptual thought, and increase the ability for the recognition of the awakened awareness through the door of its lucidly clear knowing (Brown, 2017, p. 124)

In the Indo-Tibetan model the nervous system is described in terms of a subtle microstructure that involves four neuropsychological structural-functional elements: pathways, complexes, secretions and energies. These are known as channels, wheels, drops, and winds. According to contemplative neuropsychology these structures and functions are active across ordinary disorganized reactive mind body states and the extraordinary open blissful and regulated states of awakening (Lati, 1980). The very subtle mind of pure open awakened awareness is supported structurally at the level of the central channel, a first person functional correlate of specific deep brain structures (Loizzo, 2012). The breath retention helps to access the brain stem of the nucleus ambiguous through the vagal control of cardiorespiratory rhythms. This mechanism activates a mammalian diving reflex left from our earlier evolution (Heller et al., 1987) which gives the meditator access through meditative stimulation to the brain structure-function that supports clarifying the nondual open awareness through reducing the obsessive conceptual thinking of the frontal cortex. By enlivening the deep sensory information of the inner body, the lucidity of the awareness is brightened and the realization strengthened.

> Using the visualization of the channels and methods mentioned above, then you should practice staying in the natural state. Then using this profound skillful means, in a little while the purity and impure of [ordinary] consciousness will be separated out…. The impure dregs dissolving into the domain of space, conceptuality is removed by itself, and

awakened awareness shines forth nakedly.
As the mass of clouds of conceptual thought
becomes purified, primordial wisdom becomes
clear, just as [the sun becomes clear] when no
longer covered by clouds.... The meditative
experience stays inherently in the mind
stream. Shining forth as transparent and very
clear, without being covered by obscurations.
Druchen Gyalwa Yungdrung. (2017, p. 124)

Getting Rid of the Stains Created by the Ordinary Mind is the ninth session devoted to the stabilization of awakened awareness. The first stage of this session is Setting Up the View: since the realization is unstable the meditator is to practice continually setting up the view (space gazing) so as to repeatedly shift the basis of operation to awakened awareness more often and for longer periods of time. The second stage is *Dismantling the Ordinary Mind*: according to Shar rdza bkra shis rgyal mtshan (1859-1933), as well as Brown & Gurung (2017) dismantling entails the dismantling of the individual consciousness, the reference point that does the setting up and recognizing of awakened awareness, and all the conceptual thought associated with the process. This is akin to sGam po pa's Non-Meditation with its emphasis on amanisakara, not-taking-to-mind. Thirdly, there is Automaticity: awakened awareness is revealed as an uncreated basic quality of the mind and thus is able to sustain itself automatically at all times and in all situations.

> Third, finally after setting up and dismantling there is automaticity. After dismantling and without purposefully mediating, extend the rope of mindfulness and cultivate the state of automatic non-meditation and non-distraction. There is nothing whatsoever to meditate on. Through these pith instructions about remaining undistracted, the continuity and lucidity of awakened awareness is shown. Druchen Gyalwa Yungdrung. (2017, p.130)

The ability to stabilize the automaticity of awakened awareness leads to the tenth stage: *Taking Stainless Primordial Wisdom as the Path*. The meditator now practices maintaining and integrating this basis of operation whilst engaging in systematically more difficult circumstances. Starting with maintaining the realization whilst engaged in supportive activities such as reading texts and engaging in visualization and physical yoga practice, and leading to neutral activities such as mental reflection and analysis, the integration is completed when the practitioner can maintain awakened awareness with all negative emotional states and stressful life circumstances.

> While in this automatic state of skilled practice, learn to mix awakened awareness with all types of situations on the path such as various emotional states- fear, terror, aversion, pity, disgust, vomiting, misery, and sorrow, happiness and comfortableness, and so forth- and with cognitive states such as discursiveness, apprehension, doubt, hope and fear, suffering and all unfavorable, disagreeable or unsuitable circumstances, and then with common daily activities, such as eating, walking, moving and sitting…..All activities of body, and speech- all conduct pure and impure; virtuous and non-virtuous; good, bad or neutral- whatever you do becomes skilled practice. Druchen Gyalwa Yungdrung. (2017, p. 135)

The tenth session completes the process of liberation. At this point of development the meditator has developed the capacity to operate naturally from awakened awareness, the level of lucid, open non-dual awareness prior to the constructions of the information processing systems of perception, attention, temporal awareness, self-construct, emotion and cognition.

Bringing the liberated mind-stream to the completion of Buddhahood. The third phase of practice entitled, the *Practical Guide for Liberation, Reaching the End*, begins with the automaticity of awakened awareness as the start and then culminates in the maturity of buddhahood (Brown, 2017). In the eleventh session, *Subduing the Newly Arising Habitual Karmic Propensities During the Night*, the practitioner learns methods focused on maintaining awakened awareness into sleep and dreaming. This is known as the practice of sleep and dream sleep yoga.

Sleep yoga is the first practice to be developed and this entails maintaining the realization of awakened awareness whilst in the formless state of deep dreamless sleep. According to the tradition bringing awareness into the state of deep sleep is the transformation of the most ignorant substrate of consciousness, and parallels the capacity to maintain awareness throughout the dying process (Wangyal, 1998).

> The best practitioner mixes concentration meditation with sleep and remains mindful right into entering into sleep and recognizes awakened awareness throughout sleep. Druchen Gyalwa Yungdrung. (2017, p. 138)

The second practice, *Mastery*, is Dream yoga, the process of maintaining awakened awareness while in the dreamscape and simultaneously engaging in activities that deconstruct the deep beliefs that have been structured based on awareness's identification with a life time as an individual human (Wangyal, 2004, & Norbu, 1992). According to Buddhist psychology the dream state is the most responsive state from which to transform the deep habitual karmic tendencies that have built up in the mind (Norbu, 1992). Once practitioners recognize that they are lucidly awake in the dream state they then engage in visualization practice changing themselves into a meditation deity and their body and limbs into the assembly of deities belonging to the mandala mansion of the deity. Meditators are essentially deconstructing their world and self-image at a very deep level. The ability to transform the self from one structure to another reveals a lack of self-reification and recognition of the emptiness or constructed nature of all self-images. As such these dream practices are the method through which all deluded appearances are mastered (Brown and Gurung, 2017). Practitioners continue by engaging in actions impossible in the waking state such as walking through walls, flying, breathing underwater, walking through fire, becoming transparent, moving through mountains, and relating to fearful scenarios with mindfulness cognizant of the illusory nature of the show (Brown and Gurung, 2017).

The third sub phase of the eleventh session is *Multiplying*. Since the dream state is a virtual mind created environment only limited by the mind, the practitioner engages in emanating multiple copies of themselves throughout different dreamscapes, transforming elements, taming all dream being, and transforming their own emotional states into dream figures.

> The mental body that is made of habitual karmic tendencies can manifest as anything once you have mastery over it. By just being mindful of this mental body it already transforms itself. The mind, the agent of movement, is able to go where it is guided. If these three occur- 1) just by imagining it, you can go to whatever place you want, 2) whatever appears like this, you are able to change into anything, and 3) whatever this mental body thinks to do, it becomes that- then all deluded dream-like appearances are brought into the path. Druchen Gyalwa Yungdrung. (2017, p. 141)

Having thoroughly understood the illusory constructed nature of dream appearances as the lively creative expression of mind the meditator deepens the realization in session twelve, *Training Liveliness with Respect to Appearances During the Day*, and session thirteen, *Taking Conceptual Thought as the Path*. The recognition of appearance as the lively energetic expression of the primordial mind is brought to the waking state. All sights, sounds, smells, tastes, sensations, and thought are recognized as the lively expression of awakened awareness until the meditator can no longer be lost in ordinary experience. This continuous uninterrupted non-meditation views all perceptions as 'self-arising and self-liberating' (*rang shar ran grol*).

> This practice entails holding the view of the inseparable pair- the vast expanse of the universal ground simultaneously to viewing whatever arises within that vast expanse as the liveliness of awakened awareness- and then whatever arises goes its own way and therefore is immediately liberated leaving no trace. When there is no mental engagement whatsoever, such that whatever arises is left completely in its own way and therefore is immediately liberated immediately leaving no trace. When there is no mental engagement the immediately arising event does not form a karmic memory trace.

Holding this view established the conditions for the automatic release of all ripening habitual karmic tendencies- a process known as dharmadhatu exhaustion. (Brown, 2017, p.144)

The fruition of the process of dharmadhatu exhaustion brought about by the practice of *self-arising and self-liberating* (*rang shar ran grol*) is that all past karmic imprints stored over this life-time and received by virtue of having a human body with ancestral, cultural, and racial conditioning, are released over time. The process is completed when the mind becomes *stainless* (drimed), as all negative mind states have been purified, and all the positive qualities of mind (kindness, generosity, patience etc.)

The next session, session fourteen, *Continuously Pointing Out* begins when through the stability of realization and the momentum resultant from dharmadhatu exhaustion the intrinsic intelligence of awakened awareness continuously reveals the rest of the path to itself by itself. The meditation instruction is to know the mind's limitlessness beyond the limitations of the individual and external reality. This focus on the limitlessness leads to the direct realization that all archetypal buddhafields, all realms, and times are always already right here (Brown, & Gurung, 2017).

Brown (2017) describes how the realization goes through a three-step process of stabilization. First, there is the extended practice of the formal meditation and post-meditation:

> Staying uninterruptedly in a state of one-pointedness (on the view of the inseparable pair of unbound space and awakened awareness) across the three gates of body, speech and mind, is concentrated evenness; conduct throughout the various activities and behavior is post-meditation. Druchen Gyalwa Yungdrung. (2017, p. 170)

As the meditation matures second phase known as *heroic state meditation* begins:

> By that automatic state, there won't be even the slightest distinction between holding or not holding mindfulness, sleeping and waking, and being distracted or undistracted from the real nature of the mind. There is still a slight distinction between the times of meditation and post-mediation, clarity and lack of clarity, or increasing or decreasing of the meditation. Druchen Gyalwa Yungdrung (2017, p. 174)

This process culminates in *mastery meditation*.

Freed from the slightest metacognitive activity to maintain the meditation, the state becomes undistractable, and there is no difference between meditation and post-meditation.

> You never leave a state wherein the meditation never becomes distracted nor grasps at anything, and there is no difference whatsoever between meditation and non-meditation. Meditation and non-meditation become inseparable. Whatever your activity may be, you never move from awakened awareness. Holding or not holding mindfulness, going or not going to sleep-everything- becomes inseparable from the real nature of the mind in very single instant. Druchen Gyalwa Yungdrung (2017, p. 175)

This fruition manifests itself in realization of three dimensions: the realization of the enlightened bodies, the primordial wisdoms, and enlightened activity in the form of skillful means, great compassion/loving kindness, and omniscience.

The Three Bodies

The three enlightened bodies, Dharmakaya, sambhogakaya, and nirmanakya, (kaya) can also be translated as fields or dimensions of the enlightened mind. The Dharmakaya, dimension of the teachings, (or Bon sku in Bon) is the field or dimension of the unbounded, unborn, uncreated open ground of reality akin to the purification of deep sleep. The samabhogakaya, enjoyment dimension, arising from within the open field of the Dharmakaya, is the field of light in the form of brilliant, primordial, lucid, lively awareness, and its nondual manifestations in the form of pure geometric archetypal light fields (Buddha realms) akin to the purification of the dreaming mind. The nirmanakaya, emanation dimension, represents the infinite display of reality all expressing itself for the compassionate intention to awaken all beings to their true nature as radiant self-arising-self-liberating liveliness akin to the purification of the waking mind. This realization can be seen through the lens of the 12-link cycle of conditioned dependent origination that we examined in chapter two as 12 links of enlightened fruition (see below Figure 2).

Figure 2
Twelve links of Enlightened Fruition

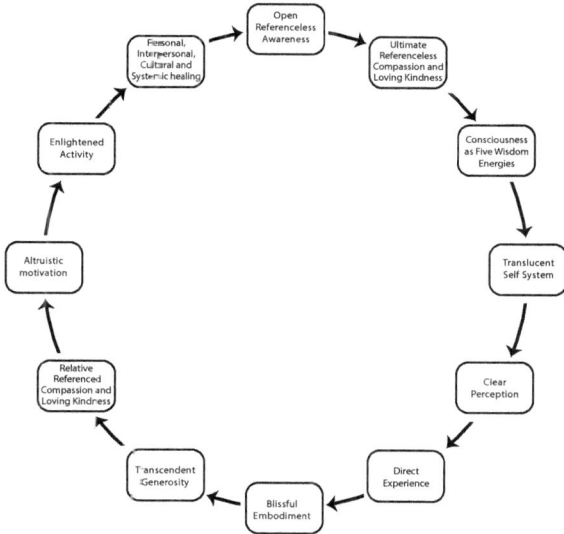

THE FIVE PRIMORDIAL WISDOMS

The primordial wisdoms describe how the human mind operates once it is gone through the purification process of the contemplative path, and arrived at the fruition of buddhahood (Thrangu, 2011).

With the permanent eradication of unconscious confusion and ignorance, the sense of reality's solidity dissolves and the *buddha* (awakened) wisdom of all pervading space wisdom reveals itself.

> With the transformation of the all-base consciousness (universal unconscious) delusion is abandoned and insight into the true nature, the dharmadhatu, the inherent nature of the completely pure aspect of the delusion based appearance is attained…It corresponds to the primordial nature that knows the nature of reality exactly as it is. Thrangu (2011, p. 61)

Through the purification of anger and default consciousness the *Vajra* (diamond) wisdom mirror-like clarity becomes operational. This primordial awareness is able to simultaneously recognize the completely pure space wisdom of the dharmadhatu whilst also clearly seeing and understanding the dualistic deluded mind of others. The mirror-like awareness has the capacity to know non-dual non-conceptual openness and simultaneously understand how the cause and effect of duality functions.

> From the perspective of mirror-like primordial awareness, a Buddha, knows all of the personal, delusion-based appearances of all

sentient beings, their individual differences, their negative conditions and their sufferings. This is the function of mirror like primordial awareness of a Buddha. Thrangu Rinpoche (2011, p. 62)

Through the transformation of hedonic tone, the feeling of like and dislike towards others, and the grasping emotion of pride associated with self-reification, the *Ratna* (jewel) wisdom of equanimity becomes operational. This wisdom-awareness views all appearance within non-dual openness as equal and does not develop attachments to any specific content. Therefore, the discrimination between the differences between self and other dissolves and every being is felt as being of equal worth.

Through the transformation of mental formations and desire the *Padma* (lotus) wisdom of discriminatory awareness balances the wisdom of equanimity. In this way a Buddha does not fall into a lack of discriminating good and bad actions despite their equality within the field of awareness. Discriminating primordial awareness is not clouded by projection and perceives the unique differences of specific individuals and circumstances spontaneously and simultaneous with primordial openness.

Through the transformation of the perceptual system and jealousy, the *Karma (action) all-accomplishing wisdom* of purified executive functioning becomes operational. It is through this wisdom that undeluded decision-making, and action, can be expressed without hesitation as spontaneous appropriate conduct in the service of alleviating the suffering of interdependent life. Such activity is described as being *wrathful* in that it destroys the outer and inner obstacles of beings (Thrangu, 2011). This powerful awareness allows for a buddha's service activity of energized and appropriate teaching and counseling.

The operation of the five wisdoms allow a buddha, motivated by great compassion and loving kindness, to integrate his or her understanding of the path, the needs of individual beings, and the application of skillful techniques into an appropriate therapeutic intervention. The true fruition of Buddhist contemplative psychology is the development and flowering of heroic altruists devoted to serving the greater social good (Loizzo, 2012).

CONCLUSION

$\mathcal{L}$ooking at the underlying architecture of the Mahamudra and rDzogchen systems presented a common pattern emerges. In the process of contemplative psychological development it is necessary to first recognize, and then stabilize, a basis of operation before it can integrate the relative activity of body, speech and mind into a non-dual realization. For instance, in the Mahamudra the practitioner realizes the very subtle timeless mind, and once that view is established as the basis of operation then the relative activity of mind is allowed to arise within that timeless very subtle spacious field. The four yoga Mahamudra tradition has a greater differentiation of levels of metacognitive operation prior to awakened awareness than the A Khrid system. As such the four-yoga Mahamudra articulates the process of establishing a basis of operation and its non-dual function at the subtle (emptiness of phenomena/dreamer and dream), very subtle (one taste reverse samadhi), and the awakened level of mind. Daniel Brown explains in his translation of the A Khrid pith instructions that the unique feature of the A Khrid system is its quickness and single-minded pursuit of awakening through using very intense comprehensive methods (Brown, 2017). As such, the A Khrid system cuts to the root of the issue and focuses on establishing awakened awareness, and then articulates in much greater detail the practice and stabilization of its non-dual liveliness. What can be seen in the Mahamudra and rDzogchen is a process intrinsic to human development. There is an orientation to a whole field (subtle, very subtle, awakened) that leads to the recognition of a metacognitive basis of operation. That new basis of operation then orients to the perceptual and cognitive expressions within the whole phenomenological field whilst simultaneously recognizing objects as an integrated expression of that field. When integrated, the intention shifts to establishing the next whole field as a basis of psychological operation. Because the whole fields are nested contexts (the awakened level includes, the very subtle, the subtle, and the coarse) this allows for the A Khrid system to cut through to the awakened level and in the non-dual integration of liveliness all prior levels of development are subsumed.

In closing may this short treatise help to orient you to the further reaches of our shared human potential, including that of Buddhahood. There is a much larger conversation unfolding with regard to the integration of Western psychology and the world's great contemplative traditions. May this offering serve as a piece of that larger dialogue.

BIBLIOGRAPHY

Achard, J. L. (2012). *The instructions on the primordial A.* Kathmandu, Nepal: Vajra Publications.

Adeu, R (2011). *Freedom in Bondage: The Life and Teachings of Adeu Rinpoche.* Berkeley, CA: Atlantic Books

Alexander, C. N., Davies, J. L., Dixon, C. A., Dillbeck, M. C., Druker, S. M., Oetzel, R. M., & Orme-Johnson, D. W. (1990). *Growth of higher stages of consciousness: Maharishi's Vedic psychology of human development* (286-341). Higher Stages of Human Development. Oxford, UK: Oxford University Press.

Arlin, P. K. (1984). Adolescent and adult thought: A structural interpretation. In M. L. Commons, F. A. Richards, & C. Armon (Eds.), *Beyond formal operations: Late adolescent and adult cognitive development* (258-271). New York, NY: Praeger.

Armon, C. (1984). Ideals of the good life and moral judgment: Ethical reasoning across the lifespan. In M. L. Commons, F. A. Richards, & C. Armon (Eds.), *Beyond formal operations: Late adolescent and adult cognitive development* (357-380). New York, NY: Praeger.

Bandura, A. (1961). Psychotherapy as a learning process. *Psychological Bulletin, 58*(2), 143-159. doi: 10.1037/h0040672

Bandura, A. (1997). *Self-efficacy: The exercise of control.* Boston, MA: Macmillian

Basseches, M. A. (1984). Dialectical thinking as a metasystematic form of cognitive organization. In M. L. Commons, F. A. Richards, & C. Armon (Eds.), *Beyond formal operations: Late adolescent and adult cognitive development* (216-257). New York, NY: Praeger.

Batchelor, S. (1997). *Buddhism without beliefs: A contemporary guide to awakening.* London: Penguin Group.

Bateman, A. W., & Fonagy, P. (2012). *Handbook of mentalizing in mental health practice.* Washington, DC: American PsychiA Khridc Publishing, Inc.

Bhattacharya, R. (2003). Science and philosophy in early Buddhism. *Anvīkṣā, 24,* 13-22.

Benack, S. (1984). Postformal epistemologies and the growth of empathy. In M. L. Commons, F. A. Richards, & C. Armon (Eds.), *Beyond formal operations: Late adolescent and adult cognitive development* (340-356). New York, NY: Praeger

Bennett, C. S. (2006). Attachment theory and research applied to the conceptualization and treatment of pathological narcissism. *Clinical Social Work Journal*, *34*(1), 45-60.

Benson, H., Beary, J. F., & Carol, M. P. (1974). The relaxation response. *Psychiatry*, *37(1)*, 37-46.

Berzin, A. (n.d.) *Study Buddhism: Project of Berzin Archives* [Website]. Retrieved from www.studybuddhism.com

Bohart, A. (1983). Detachment: A variable common to many psychotherapies? Paper presented at the 63rd Annual Convention of the Western Psychological Association, San Francisco, CA.

Blumentritt, T. L. (2011). Is higher better? A review and analysis of the correlates of postconventional ego development. In A. H. Pfaffenberger, P. W. Marko, & A. Combs (Eds.), *The postconventional personality: Assessing, researching, and theorizing higher development* (153-162).

Borkowski, J. G., Chan, L. K., & Muthukrishna, N. (2000). A process-oriented model of metacognition: Links between motivation and executive functioning. In Gregory Schraw & James C (Eds.), *Issues in the Measurement of Metacognition*. Lincoln, NE: Buros Institute of Mental Measurements (1-41).

Brewer, J. A., Garrison, K. A., & Whitfield-Gabrieli, S. (2013). What about the "self" is processed in the posterior cingulate cortex? *Frontiers in Human*

Neuroscience, 7, Article ID 647. doi: 10.3389/fnhum.2013.00647

Brown, A. (1987). Metacognition, executive control, self-regulation, and other more mysterious mechanisms. In F. E. Weinert, R. Kluwe (Eds.), *Metacognition, motivation, and understanding* (65-116). Hillsdale, NJ: L. Erlbaum Associates.

Brown, D. P. et al. (2016). *Attachment disturbances in adults: Treatment for comprehensive repair.* New York, NY: W. W. Norton & Company, Inc.

Brown, D. (1986). The stages of meditation in cross-cultural perspective. In K. Wilber, J. Engler, & D. Brown (Eds.), *Transformations of consciousness: Conventional and contemplative perspectives on development* (219-283). Boston, MA: New Science Library.

Brown, D. (2006). *Pointing out the great way: The stages of meditation in the mahamudra tradition.* Somerville, MA: Wisdom Publications.

Brown, D. (2016). *The stages of Tibetan great completion meditation, adult post-formal cognitive & metacognitive development: Implications for mental health and optimal development.* Slide Presentation at Harvard Peak Performance, Cape Cod.

Brown, D. & Gurung, (2017). *Pith instructions for A khrid rdzogs chen* San Francisco, CA: Bright Alliance.

Brown, K. W., Ryan, R. M., & Creswell, J. D. (2007). Mindfulness: Theoretical foundations and evidence for its salutary effects. *Psychological inquiry*, *18*(4), 211-237.

Bruner, J. S. (1990). *Acts of meaning.* Cambridge, MA: Harvard University Press.

Bru rGyal ba G.yunG drunG (2017). *Pith instructions for A khrid rdzogs chen* (D. P. Brown & G. S. Gurung, Trans.). San Francisco, CA: Bright Alliance

Buswell Jr, R. E., & Lopez Jr, D. S. (2013). *The Princeton Dictionary of Buddhism.* Princeton University Press.

Butler, A. C., Chapman, J. E., Forman, E. M., & Beck, A. T. (2006). The empirical status of cognitive-behavioral therapy: A review of meta-analyses. *Clinical Psychology Review, 26*(1), 17-31. doi: 10.1016/j.cpr.2005.07.003

Chagmé, K. (1997). *A spacious path to freedom: Practical instructions on the union of mahamudra and atiyoga* (G. Rinpoche, commentary; B. A. Wallace, Trans.). Ithaca, NY: Snow Lion Publications.

Chagmé, K. (2000). *Naked awareness* (G. Rinpoche, commentary; B. A. Wallace, Trans.). Ithaca, NY: Snow Lion Publications.

Chögyam, N., & Déchen, K. (2002). *Roaring silence: Discovering the mind of Rdzogchen.* Boston, MA: Shambhala Publications.

Christopher, J. C. (1996). Counseling's inescapable moral visions. *Journal of Counseling & Development, 75*(1), 17-25. doi: 10.1002/j.1556-6676.1996.tb02310.x

Christopher, J. C. (1999). Situating psychological well-being: Exploring the cultural roots of its theory and research. *Journal of Counseling & Development, 77*(2), 141-152. doi: 10.1002/j.1556-6676.1999.tb02434.x

Christopher, J. C., Wendt, D. C., Marecek, J., & Goodman, D. M. (2014). Critical cultural awareness: Contributions to a globalizing psychology. *American Psychologist, 69*(7), 645-655. doi: 10.1037/a0036851

Cohn, L. D., & Westenberg, P. M. (2004). Intelligence and maturity: meta-analytic evidence for the incremental and discriminant validity of Loevinger's measure of ego development. *Journal of Personality and Social Psychology, 86*(5), 760-772.

Colman, A. M. (2015). *A dictionary of psychology.* New York, NY: Oxford University Press, USA.

Commons, M. L., Richards, F. A. & Kuhn, D. (1982). Systematic and metasystematic reasoning: A case for levels of reasoning beyond Piaget's stage of formal operations. *Child Development, 53*(4), 1058-1069. doi: 10.2307/1129147

Commons, M. L., & Richards, F. A. (2002). Four postformal stages. In J. Demick, C. Andreoletti (Eds.), *Handbook of adult development* (199-219). Boston, MA: Springer. doi: 10.1007/978-1-4615-0617-1_11

Commons, M. L. & Ross, S. N. (2008). What postformal thought is, and why it matters. *World Futures: The Journal of New Paradigm Research, 64*(5-7), 321-329. doi: 10.1080/02604020802301139

Commons, M. L., & Chen, S. J. (2014). Advances in the model of hierarchical complexity (MHC). *Behavioral Development Bulletin, 19*(4), 37-50. doi: 10.1037/h0101080

Cook-Greuter, S. R. (1999). *Postautonomous ego development: A study of its nature and measurement* (Doctoral dissertation, Harvard Graduate School of Education). Retrieved from https://www.amazon.com/Postautonomous-Ego-Development-Measurement-Dissertation/dp/1450725155

Cook-Greuter, S. R., & Soulen, J. (2007). The developmental perspective in integral counseling. *Counseling and Values, 51*(3), 180-192. doi: 10.1002/j.2161-007X.2007.tb00077.x

Cook-Greuter, S. (2013). *Nine levels of increasing embrace in ego development: A full-spectrum theory of vertical growth and meaning making.* Retrieved from http://www.cook-greuter.com

Cook-Greuter, S. (2005). *Ego development: Nine levels of increasing embrace.* Retrieved from http://www.cook-greuter.com

Cousins, L. S. (1996). The dating of the historical Buddha:

A review article. *Journal of the Royal Asiatic society, 6*(1), 57-63. doi: 10.1017/S1356186300014760

Cross, D. R., & Paris, S. G. (1988). Developmental and instructional analyses of children's metacognition and reading comprehension. *Journal of Educational Psychology, 80*(2), 131-142. doi: 10.1037/0022-0663.80.2.131

Dalai Lama, Berzin, A. (1997). *The Gelug/Kagyu tradition of mahamudra.* Ithica, NY: Snow Lion Publications.

Dalai Lama (2000). *Rdzogchen: heart essence of the great perfection.* Boston, MA: Shambhala.

Dalai Lama (2005). *The universe in a single atom: The convergence of science and spirituality.* New York, NY: Harmony.

Dalai Lama (1999). Sage's *h*armonious *s*ong of *t*ruth [poem]. Retrieved from http://www.lotsawahouse.org/tibetan-masters/fourteenth-dalai-lama/harmonious-song-truth

Dale, E. J. (2013). Neo-Piagetian Transpersonal psychology: a new perspective *Journal of Transpersonal Psychology, 45*(2).

Das, S. (2007). *Buddha is as Buddha does: The ten original practices for enlightened living.* San Fransisco, CA: HarperSanFrancisco.

Davidson, R. (2012). *The emerging field of contemplative*

neuroscience. Lecture at the Center for Compassion and Altruism Research and Education (CCARE) at Stanford University. Retrieved from http://www.mindful.org/the-emerging-field-of-contemplative-neuroscience/

De Chardin, P. T. (2004). *The future of man.* Image. New York, NY: Doubleday.

Deikman, A. (1982). *The observing self.* Boston, MA: Beacon Press.

Dictionary, O. E. (2007). Oxford English dictionary online.

Demetriou, A. (1990). Structural and developmental relations between formal and postformal capacities: Towards a comprehensive theory of adolescent and adult cognitive development. In M. L. Commons, C. Armon, L. Kohlberg, F. A. Richards, T. A. Grotzer, & J. D. Sinnott (Eds.), *Adult development: Models and methods in the study of adolescent and adult thought, Vol. 2.* (147-174). New York, NY: Praeger Publishers.

Desmarais, M. M. (2008). Changing minds: Mind, consciousness and identity in Patañjali's yoga-sūtra and cognitive neuroscience. New Delhi, India: Motilal Banarsidass.

DeMartino, R. J. (1991). Karen Horney, Daisetz T. Suzuki, and Zen Buddhism. *The American Journal of Psychoanalysis, 51*(3), 267-283.

DiPerna, D. (2015). Streams of wisdom: an advanced guide to integral spiritual development. Occidental, CA: Bright Alliance.

Dobson, K. S. (2013). The science of CBT: Toward a metacognitive model of change? *Behavior Therapy, 44*(2), 224-227. doi: 10.1016/j.beth.2009.08.003

Dobson, K. S. (Ed.). (2010). *Handbook of cognitive-behavioral therapies, 3rd edition.* New York, NY: Guilford Press.

Dorjee, D. (2016). Defining contemplative science: the metacognitive self-regulatory capacity of the mind, context of meditation practice and modes of existential awareness. *Frontiers in psychology, 7*, 1788.

Dorjee, D. (2013). *Mind, brain and the path to happiness: A guide to Buddhist mind training and the neuroscience of meditation.* New York, NY: Routledge.

Dowman, K. (2017). *Everything is light: The circle of total illumination.* Katmandu, Nepal: Rdzogchen Now! Books.

De Wit, H. F., & Baird, M. L. (1991). *Contemplative psychology.* Pittsburgh, PA: Duquesne University Press.

Duff, T. (2011). *SGam po pa teaches essence mahamudra: Interviews with his heart disciples, vol. 1.* Kathmandu, Nepal: Padma Karpo Translation Committee.

Efklides, A. (2006). Metacognition and affect: What can

metacognitive experiences tell us about the learning process? *Educational research review, 1*(1), 3-14.

Eisenberg, N., Valiente, C., & Eggum, N. D. (2010). Self-regulation and school readiness. *Early Education and Development, 21*(5), 681-698.

Engler, J. (1984). Therapeutic aims in psychotherapy and meditation: Developmental stages in the representation of self. *The Journal of Transpersonal Psychology, 16*(1), 25.

Elias, M. (2009, June 7). Mindfulness' meditation being used in hospitals and schools. *USA Today*. Retrieved from http://usatoday30.usatoday.com/news/health/2009-06-07-meditate_N.html

Fischer, K. W., Hand, H. H., & Russell, S. (1984). The development of abstractions in adolescents and adulthood. In M. L. Commons, F. A. Richards, & C. Armon (Eds.), *Beyond formal operations: Late adolescent and adult cognitive development* (43-73). New York: Praeger.

Fernandez-Duque, D., Baird, J. A., & Posner, M. I. (2000). Executive attention and metacognitive regulation. *Consciousness and cognition, 9*(2), 288-307.

Flavell, J. H., & Wellman, H. M. (1975). "Metamemory". National Inst. of Child Health and Human Development (NIH), Bethesda, MD.; National Science Foundation, Washington, DC.

Flavell, J. H. (1979). Metacognition and cognitive monitoring: A new area of cognitive–developmental inquiry. *American Psychologist, 34*(10), 906.

Fonagy, P., Target, M., & Gergely, G. (2000). Attachment and borderline personality disorder: A theory and some evidence. *PsychiA Khridc Clinics, 23*(1), 103-122.

Fonagy, P., & Allison, E. (2016). Psychic reality and the nature of consciousness. *The International Journal of Psychoanalysis, 97*(1), 5-24.

Fonagy, P., Gergely, G., & Target, M. (2007). The parent–infant dyad and the construction of the subjective self. *Journal of Child Psychology and Psychiatry, 48*(3-4), 288-328.

Forman, M. D. (2012). *Guide to integral psychotherapy, A: complexity, integration, and spirituality in practice.* Albany, NY: SUNY Press.

Freud, S. (1977). *Introductory lectures on psychoanalysis.* New York, NY: Norton & Company.

Freud, S. (1990) *The ego and the id.* New York, NY: Norton & Company.

Freud, S. (2010). *Civilization and its discontents.* New York, NY: W.W. Norton & Company.

Fromm, E., Suzuki, D.T. & De Martino, R. (1960). *Zen Buddhism and psychoanalysis.* Oxford, England: Harper.

Gendlin, E. T. (2012). *Focusing-oriented psychotherapy:*

A manual of the experiential method. NewYork ,NY: Guilford Press.

Gilmore, J. M., & Durkin, K. (2001). A critical review of the validity of ego development theory and its measurement. *Journal of Personality Assessment, 77*(3), 541-567.

Goodall, K., Trejnowska, A., & Darling, S. (2012). The relationship between dispositional mindfulness, attachment security and emotion regulation. *Personality and Individual Differences, 52*(5), 622-626.

Grof, S., & Bennett, H. Z. (1993). *The holotropic mind: The three levels of human consciousness and how they shape our lives.* San Francisco, CA: HarperSanFrancisco.

Grossenbacher, P. G., & Quaglia, J. T. (2017). Contemplative Cognition A More Integrative Framework for Advancing Mindfulness and Meditation Research. *Mindfulness, 8*(6), 1580-1593.

Guenther, H. V. & Kawamura, L. S. (1975). *Mind in Buddhist psychology.* Emeryville, CA: Dharma.

Guenther, H. V. (1989). *From reductionism to creativity: rDzogs-chen and the new sciences of mind.* Boston, MA: Shambhala.

Gyatso, S. D. (2016). *The Mirror of Beryl: A Historical Introduction to Tibetan Medicine* (Vol. 28). New York, NY:Simon and Schuster.

Hanh, T. N. (1999). *The heart of the Buddha's teaching.* New York, NY: Random House.

Hayes, S. C., Villatte, M., Levin, M., & Hildebrandt, M. (2011). Open, aware, and active: Contextual approaches as an emerging trend in the behavioral and cognitive therapies. *Annual Review of Clinical Psychology, 7,* 141-168.

Hayes, S. C., Levin, M. E., Plumb-Vilardaga, J., Villatte, J. L., & Pistorello, J. (2013). Acceptance and commitment therapy and contextual behavioral science: Examining the progress of a distinctive model of behavioral and cognitive therapy. *Behavior Therapy, 44*(2), 180-198.

Hayes, S. C., Wilson, K. G., Gifford, E. V., Follette, V. M., & Strosahl, K. (1996). Experiential avoidance and behavioral disorders: A functional dimensional approach to diagnosis and treatment. *Journal of Consulting and Clinical Psychology, 64*(6), 1152

Heller, H. C., Elsner, R., & Rao, N. (1987). Voluntary hypometabolism in an Indian yogi. *Journal of Thermal Biology, 12*(2), 171-173.

Herzberg, K. N., Sheppard, S. C., Forsyth, J. P., Credé, M., Earleywine, M., & Eifert, G. H. (2012). The Believability of Anxious Feelings and Thoughts Questionnaire (BAFT): A psychometric evaluation of cognitive fusion in a nonclinical and highly anxious community sample. *Psychological Assessment, 24*(4), 877.

Higgins, D. (2008). On the development of the non-mentation (amanasikāra) doctrine in Indo-Tibetan Buddhism. *Journal of the International Association of Buddhist Studies, 29*(2), 255-303.

Hixon, L. (1993). *Mother of the Buddhas: Meditations on the prajnaparamita sutra.* Wheaton, IL: Quest Books.

Hofmann, S. G , Asmundson, G. J., & Beck, A. T. (2013). The science of cognitive therapy. *Behavior Therapy, 44*(2), 199-212.

Hofmann, S. G., Sawyer, A. T., Witt, A. A., & Oh, D. (2010). The effect of mindfulness-based therapy on anxiety and depression: A meta-analytic review. *Journal of Consulting and Clinical Psychology, 78*(2), 169-183.

Ingersoll, R. E., & Rak, C. F. (2015). *Psychopharmacology for mental health professionals: An integrative approach.* Boston, MA: Brooks Cole.

Irving, L. M., Snyder, C. R., Cheavens, J., Gravel, L., Hanke, J., Hilberg, P., & Nelson, N. (2004). The relationships between hope and outcomes at the pretreatment, beginning, and later phases of psychotherapy. *Journal of Psychotherapy Integration, 14*(4), 419-433.

Ingersoll, R E., & Zeitler, D. M. (2010). *Integral psychotherapy: Inside out/outside in.* Albany: NY: SUNY Press.

Kabat-Zinn, J. (2009). *Wherever you go, there you are: Mindfulness meditation in everyday life.* New York, NY: Hachette Books.

Jankowski, T., & Holas, P. (2014). Metacognitive model of mindfulness. *Consciousness and cognition, 28*, 64-80.

James, W. (1890). *The principles of psychology.* New York, NY: Holt and Company.

James, W. (1985). *The varieties of religious experience.* Cambridge, MA: Harvard University Press.

Jespersen, K., Kroger, J., & Martinussen, M. (2013). Identity status and ego development: A meta-analysis. *Identity, 13*(3), 228-241.

Kapoor, A., Dunn, E., Kostaki, A., Andrews, M. H., & Matthews, S. G. (2006). Fetal programming of hypothalamo-pituitary-adrenal function: prenatal stress and glucocorticoids. *The Journal of Physiology, 572*(1), 31-44.

Kelly, B. D. (2008). Buddhist psychology, psychotherapy and the brain: A critical introduction. *Transcultural Psychiatry, 45*(1), 5-30.

Kegan, R. (1995). *In over our heads: The mental demands of modern life.* Cambridge, MA: Harvard University Press.

Kegan, R. (1982). *The evolving self.* Cambridge, MA: Harvard University Press.

Keown, D. (2003). *A dictionary of Buddhism.* New York, NY: Oxford University Press, Inc.

Klonchen-pa Drimed'od-zer. (1993). *The practice of Rdzogchen..* Cambridge, MA: Snow Lion.

Kohlberg, L. (1990). Which postformal levels are stages? In M. L. Commons, C. Armon, L. Kohlberg, F. A. Richards, T. A. Grotzer, & J. D. Sinnott (Eds.), *Adult development: Models and methods in the study of adolescent and adult thought, Vol. 2.* (263-268). New York, NY: Praeger Publishers.

Koplowitz, H. (1984). A projection beyond Piaget's formal operations stage: A general system stage and a unitary stage. In M. L. Commons, A. Richards, & C. Armon (Eds.), *Beyond formal operations: vol. 1.* New York, NY: Praeger.

Kuhn, D. (2000). Theory of mind, metacognition, and reasoning: A life-span perspective. *Children's reasoning and the mind,* 301-326.

Kuhn, T. S., & Hawkins, D. (1963). The structure of scientific revolutions. *American Journal of Physics, 31*(7), 554-555.

Johnson, D. P., Penn, D. L., Fredrickson, B. L., Kring, A. M., Meyer, P. S., Catalino, L. I., & Brantley, M. (2011). A pilot study of loving-kindness meditation for the negative symptoms of schizophrenia. *Schizophrenia Research, 129*(2), 137-140.

Joiner, W. B., & Josephs, S. A. (2006). *Leadership agility: Five levels of mastery for anticipating and initiating change (vol. 307).* Marblehead, MA: John Wiley & Sons.

Jung, C. (1939) Introduction. In D. T. Suzuki, *An introduction to Zen Buddhism.* New York, NY: Grove Press.

Kabat-Zinn, J. (1990). *Full catastrophe living: Using the wisdom of your body and mind in everyday life.* New York, NY: Delacorte.

LaBerge, S. & Reheingold H. (1991) *Exploring the world of lucid dreaming.* New York: Ballantine Books.

Labouvie-Vief, G. (1980). Beyond formal operations: Uses and limits of pure logic in life-span development. *Human Development, 23*, 141-161.

Lai, E. R. (2011). *Metacognition: A literature review.* Boston, MA: Pearson.

Lamrimpa, G. (2002). *Realizing emptiness: Madhyamaka insight meditation.* Boston, MA: Snow Lion Publications.

Lancaster, B. L. (1997). On the stages of perception: Towards a synthesis of cognitive neuroscience and the Buddhist Abhidhamma tradition. *Journal of Consciousness Studies, 4*(2), 122-122.

Lilienfeld, S. O., Wood, J. M., & Garb, H. N. (2000). The scientific status of projective techniques. *Psychological Science in the Public Interest, 1*(2), 27-66.

Loevinger, J. (1966). The meaning and measurement of ego development. *American Psychologist, 21*(3), 195-206.

Loevinger, J. (1976). *Ego development: Conceptions and theories*. San Francisco, CA: Jossey-Bass.

Loevinger, J., Wessler, R., & Redmore, C. (1970). *Measuring ego development (Vol. 2)*. San Francisco, CA: Jossey-Bass.

Loevinger, J. (Ed.). (1998). *Technical foundations for measuring ego development: The Washington University sentence completion test*. New York, NY: Psychology Press.

Loizzo, J. (2011). Personal agency across generations: Evolutionary psychology or religious belief? *Sophia, 50*(3), 429-452.

Loizzo, J. (2012). *Sustainable happiness: The mind science of well-being, altruism, and inspiration*. New York, NY: Routledge.

Loizzo, J. (2014). Meditation research, past, present, and future: Perspectives from the Nalanda contemplative science tradition. *Annals of the New York Academy of Sciences, 1307*(1), 43-54.

Loizzo, J., Neale, M., & Wolf, E. J. (Eds.). (2017). *Advances in contemplative psychotherapy: Accelerating healing and transformation*. New York, NY: Taylor & Francis.

Lopez, D. S. (1998). *Prisoners of Shangri-La: Tibetan Buddhism and the west*. Chicago, IL: University of Chicago Press.

Lopez Jr., D. S. (2001). *The story of Buddhism: A concise guide to its history and teachings*. San Francisco, CA: HarperSanFrancisco

Mahoney, M. J. (1977). Reflections on the cognitive-learning trend in psychotherapy. *American Psychologist, 32*(1), 5-13.

Main, M. (1991). Metacognitive knowledge, metacognitive monitoring, and singular (coherent) vs. multiple (incoherent) models of attachment. *Attachment Across the Life Cycle,* 127-159.

Martin, D. (2001). *Unearthing Bon Treasures: Life and Contested Legacy of a Tibetan Scripture Revealer, with a General Bibliography of Bon*. Kathmandu, Nepal: Vajra Publications

Mason, L. I., & Orme-Johnson, D. W. (2010). Transcendental consciousness wakes up in dreaming and deep sleep. *International Journal of Dream Research, 3*, 28-32.

Masterpasqua, F. (2016). Mindfulness mentalizing humanism: A transtheoretical convergence. *Journal of Psychotherapy Integration, 26*(1), 5-10.

Markič, O., & Kordeš, U. (2016). Parallels between mindfulness and first-person research into consciousness. *Asian Studies, 4*(2), 153-168.

Martinez, M. E. (2006). What is metacognition? *Phi Delta Kappan, 87*(9), 696-699.

Matthews, S. G., & Phillips, D. I. (2010). Minireview: Transgenerational inheritance of the stress response: A new frontier in stress research. *Endocrinology, 151*(1), 7-13.

McMahan, D. L. (2008). *The making of Buddhist modernism.* Oxford, England: Oxford University Press.

McWilliams, S. A. (2011). Contemplating a contemporary constructivist Buddhist psychology. In G. T. Maurits (Ed.), *Review of new horizons in Buddhist psychology: Relational Buddhism for collaborative practitioners* (268-276) KweeChagrin Falls, OH: Taos Institute Publications.

Medco Health Solutions Inc. (2011). *America's state of mind report.* Retrieved from http://apps.who.int/medicinedocs/documents/s19032en/s19032en.pdf

Mezirow, J. (1990). How critical reflection triggers transformative learning. *Fostering Critical Reflection in Adulthood, 1*, 20.

Michaelson, J. (2013). *Evolving dharma: Meditation, Buddhism, and the next generation of enlightenment.* Berkeley, CA: North Atlantic Books.

Miller, L. D. (2014). *Effortless mindfulness: Genuine mental health through awakened presence.* New York, NY: Routledge.

Mipham, J. (2010). *The adornment of the middle way:*

Shantarakshita's Madhyamakalankara with commentary by Jamgon Mipham. Boston, MA: Shambhala Publications.

Namgyal, D. T. (2006). *Mahamudra: The moonlight-quintessence of mind and meditation*. New York, NY: Simon and Schuster.

National Institute of Mental Health. (2015). *Mental health among adults*. Retrieved from www.nimh.nih.gov/health/statistics/prevalence/any-mental-illness-ami-among-adults.html

Mental Health Foundation. (2010). *Mindfulness report*. London, England: Mental Health Foundation Press.

Monteiro, L. M., Musten, R. F., & Compson, J. (2015). Traditional and contemporary mindfulness: finding the middle path in the tangle of concerns. *Mindfulness, 6*(1), 1-13.

Noam, G. G., & Dill, D. L. (1991). Adult development and symptomatology. *Psychiatry, 54*(2), 208-217.

Noam, G. G., & Houlihan, J. (1990). Developmental dimensions of DSM III diagnoses in adolescent psychiA Khridc patients. *American Journal of Orthopsychiatry, 60*(3), 371-378.

Norbu, N., & Katz, M. (1992). *Dream yoga and the practice of natural light*. Ithaca, NY: Snow Lion Publications.

Norbu, T. (2006). *A cascading waterfall of nectar*. Boston, MA: Shambhala Publications.

Novy, D. M., & Francis, D. J. (1992). Psychometric properties of the Washington University Sentence Completion Test. *Educational and Psychological Measurement, 52*(4), 1029-1039.

Odajnyk, V. W. (1993). *Gathering the light: A psychology of meditation.* Boston, MA: Shambhala Publications.

O'Fallon, T. (2010a). *The evolution of the human soul: Developmental practices in spiritual guidance.* Retrieved from www.lorian.org

O'Fallon, T. (2010b). Developmental experiments in individual and collective movement to second tier. *Journal of Integral Theory & Practice, 5*(2), 149-160.

O'Fallon, T. (2010c). *The collapse of the Wilber-Combs mA Khridx: The interpenetration of the state and structure stages.* Retrieved from www.pacificintegral.com/

O'Fallon, T. (2012). *Stages: Growing up is waking up-Interpenetrating quadrants, states and structures.* Retrieved from www.pacificintegral.com

O'Fallon, T. (2013). *The senses: Demystifying awakening* Retrieved from www.pacificintegral.com

O'Fallon, T., Ramirez, V., & Fitch, G.(2013). *Causal leadership: A natural emergence from later stages of awareness.* Retrieved from www.pacificintegral.com

Pannu, J. K., & Kaszniak, A. W. (2005). Metamemory experiments in neurological populations: A review. *Neuropsychology Review, 15*(3), 105-130.

Paris, S. G., & Winograd, P. (1990). Promoting metacognition and motivation of exceptional children. *Remedial and Special Education, 11*(6), 7-15.

Paul, R., & Elder, L. (2008). *Critical thinking.* Tormales, CA: The Foundation for Critical Thinking.

Pascual-Leone, J. (1984). Attention, dialectic, and mental effort: Towards an organismic theory of life stages. In M. L. Commons, F. A. Richards, & C. Armon, (Eds.), *Beyond formal operations: Late adolescent and adult cognitive development (vol. 1)* (182-215). New York, NY: Praeger Publishers.

Piaget, J. (1951). *The psychology of intelligence.* London, England: Routledge and Kegan.

Piaget, J. (1952). *The origins of intelligence in children (vol. 8, no. 5).* New York, NY: International Universities Press.

Piaget, J. (1971). The theory of stages in cognitive development. In D. Green, R. Ford, M. P. Flamer, B. George (Eds.), *Measurement and Piaget* (1-11). New York, NY: McGraw-Hill.

Pickering, J. (2006). The first-person perspective in postmodern psychology. In D. Nauriyal, M. Drummond, & Y. Lal (Eds.), *Buddhist thought and applied psychological research* (3-19). London, England: Routledge.

Ponlop, R. D. (2003). *Wild awakening: The heart of Mahamudra and Dzogchen.* Boston, MA: Shambhala Publications.

Purser, R. E., & Milillo, J. (2015). Mindfulness revisited: A Buddhist-based conceptualization. *Journal of Management Inquiry, 24*(1), 3-24.

Purser, R. E. (2015). Clearing the muddled path of traditional and contemporary mindfulness: a response to Monteiro, Musten, and Compson. *Mindfulness, 6*(1), 23-45.

Porter, R. (2002). *Madness: A brief history.* New York, NY: Oxford University Press.

Powers, J. (2009). *A bull of a man.* Cambridge, MA: Harvard University Press.

Prebish, C. (2006). The new Panditas. *Buddhadharma: The*

Practitioner's Quarterly, Spring, 62-69.

Prebish, C. S. (1999). *Luminous passage: The practice and study of Buddhism in America.* Berkeley, CA: University of California Press.

Rāhula, W. (1974). *What the Buddha taught.* New York, NY: Grove Press.

Rahula, Walpola, Boin-Webb, Sara (trans.) (2000). *Abhidharmasamuccaya. The Compendium of the Higher Teaching by Asanga.* Fremont, CA: Asian Humanities Press.

Ray, R. A. (2002). *Indestructible truth: The living spirituality of Tibetan Buddhism.* Boston, MA: Shambhala Publications.

Ray, R. A. (1999). *Buddhist saints in India*. Oxford, England: Oxford University Press.

Reynolds, J. M. (1996). *The golden letters*. Ithaca, NY: Snow Lion.

Reynolds, J. M. (2005). *The oral tradition from Zhang-Zhung*. Kathmandu, Nepal: Vajra Publications.

Reynolds, J. (2014). *The precepts of the Dharmakaya*. Kathmandu, Nepal: Vajra Books

Rinbochay, L. (1980). *Death, intermediate state, and rebirth in Tibetan Buddhism*. Boston, MA: Shambhala Publications.

Rinpoche, C. N., Schmidt, M. B., & Kunsang, E. P. (1989). *Union of Mahamudra and Rdzogchen: A commentary on the quintessence of spiritual practice, the direct instructions of the great compassionate one*. Kathmandu, Nepal: Rangjung Yeshe Publications.

Rockwell, I. (2002). *The five wisdom energies: A Buddhist way of understanding personalities, emotions, and relationships*. Boston, MA: Shambhala Publications.

Rose, T., Loewenthal, D., & Greenwood, D. (2005). Counselling and psychotherapy as a form of learning: Some implications for practice. *British Journal of Guidance & Counselling, 33*(4), 441-456.

Riegel, K. F. (1973). Dialectic operations: The final phase of cognitive development. *Human Development, 16*, 346-370.

Ringu, T.(2017, October 27th). Retrieved from http://www. rigpawiki.org

Rogers, C. R. (1969). *Freedom to learn*. Merrill, WI: Merrill Publishing Company.

Rogers, C. R. (1959). Significant learning in therapy and in education. *Educational leadership, 16*(4), 232-242.

Rogers, C. R. (1995). What understanding and acceptance mean to me. *Journal of Humanistic Psychology, 35*(4), 7-22.

Safran, J. D., Segal, Z. V., Vallis, T. M., Shaw, B. F., & Samstag, L. W. (1993). Assessing patient suitability for short-term cognitive therapy with an interpersonal focus. *Cognitive Therapy and Research, 17*(1), 23-38.

Sagi, Y., Tavor, I., Hofstetter, S., Tzur-Moryosef, S., Blumenfeld-Katzir, T., & Assaf, Y. (2012). Learning in the fast lane: new insights into neuroplasticity. *Neuron, 73*(6), 1195-1203.

Schoenberg, P. L., Ruf, A., Churchill, J., Brown, D. P., & Brewer, J. A. (2018). Mapping complex mind states: EEG neural substrates of meditative unified compassionate awareness. *Consciousness and Cognition, 57*, 41-53.

Schraw, G. (1998). Promoting general metacognitive awareness. *Instructional science, 26*(1), 113-125.

Schneider, W. (2008). The development of metacognitive

knowledge in children and adolescents: Major trends and implications for education. *Mind, Brain, and Education, 2*(3), 114-121.

Schraw, G., Crippen, K. J., & Hartley, K. (2006). Promoting self-regulation in science education: Metacognition as part of a broader perspective on learning. *Research in Science Education, 36*(1), 111-139.

Schwartz, R. C. (1997). *Internal family systems therapy*. New York, NY: Guilford Press.

Segall, M. H., Lonner, W. J., & Berry, J. W. (1998). Cross-cultural psychology as a scholarly discipline: On the flowering of culture in behavioral research. *American Psychologist, 53*(10), 1101-1110.

Segall, S. R. (2003). Psychotherapy practice as Buddhist practice. In S. R. Segall (Ed.), *Encountering Buddhism: Western psychology and Buddhist teachings* (165-178). Albany, NY: SUNY Press.

Seligman, M. E. (1995). The effectiveness of psychotherapy: The Consumer Reports study. *American Psychologist, 50*(12), 965-974.

Semerari, A., Carcione, A., Dimaggio, G., Falcone, M., Nicolò, G., Procacci, M., & Alleva, G. (2003). How to evaluate metacognitive functioning in psychotherapy? The metacognition assessment scale and its applications. *Clinical Psychology & Psychotherapy, 10*(4), 238-261.

Semerari, A., Cucchi, M., Dimaggio, G., Cavadini, D.,

Carcione, A., Battelli, V., & Ronchi, P. (2012). The development of the Metacognition Assessment interview: instrument description, factor structure and reliability in a non-clinical sample. *Psychiatry Research, 200*(2), 890-895.

Shapiro, S. L., & Carlson, L. E. (2009). *The art and science of mindfulness: Integrating mindfulness into psychology and the healing professions.* Washington, DC: American Psychological Association Press.

Shaver, P. R., Lavy, S., Saron, C. D., & Mikulincer, M. (2007). Social foundations of the capacity for mindfulness: An attachment perspective. *Psychological Inquiry, 18*(4), 264-271.

Sherab, R. K. (1995). *Profound Buddhism: From Hinayana to Vajrayana.* San Francisco, CA: ClearPoint Press.

Shonin, E., Van Gordon, W., & Griffiths, M. D. (2014). The emerging role of Buddhism in clinical psychology: Toward effective integration. *Psychology of Religion and Spirituality, 6*(2), 123-137.

Shonin, E., Van Gordon, W., & Griffiths, M. D. (2013). Mindfulness-based interventions: Towards mindful clinical integration. *Frontiers in Psychology, 4,* (194), 1-4.

Smetham, G. P. (2010). Bohm's implicate order, Wheeler's participatory universe, Stapp's mindful universe, Zurek's quantum Darwinism and the Buddhist mind-only ground consciousness. *Journal of Consciousness Exploration & Research, 1*(8), 1048-69.

Smith , Malcom (2016). Buddhahood in This Life, The Great Commentary by Vimalamitra. Boston, MA: Wisdom Books.

Snyder, R., Shapiro, S., & Treleaven, D. (2012). Attachment theory and mindfulness. *Journal of Child and Family Studies, 21*(5), 709-717.

Soler, J., Valdepérez, A., Feliu-Soler, A., Pascual, J. C., Portella, M. J., Martín-Blanco, A., & Pérez, V. (2012). Effects of the dialectical behavioral therapy-mindfulness module on attention in patients with borderline personality disorder. *Behaviour Research and Therapy, 50*(2), 150-157.

Sullivan, H.S. (1968) *The interpersonal theory of psychiatry.* NewYork, NY: Norton

Tarricone, P. (2011). *The taxonomy of metacognition.* New York, NY: Psychology Press.

Teasdale, J. D., Segal, Z. V., Williams, J. M. G., Ridgeway, V. A., Soulsby, J. M., & Lau, M. A. (2000). Prevention of relapse/recurrence in major depression by mindfulness-based cognitive therapy. *Journal of Consulting and Clinical psychology, 68*(4), 615-623.

Teasdale, J. D. (1999). Metacognition, mindfulness and the modification of mood disorders. *Clinical Psychology & Psychotherapy, 6*(2), 146-155.

Teasdale, J. D., Moore, R. G., Hayhurst, H., Pope, M., Williams, S., & Segal, Z. V. (2002). Metacognitive awareness and prevention of relapse in depression: Empirical evidence. *Journal of Consulting and Clinical Psychology, 70*(2), 275- 287.

Tervalon, M., & Murray-Garcia, J. (1998). Cultural humility versus cultural competence: A critical distinction in defining physician training outcomes in multicultural education. *Journal of Health Care for the Poor and Underserved, 9*(2), 117-125.

Thrangu, K. (2011). *Everyday consciousness and primordial awareness*. Boston, MA: Shambhala Publications.

Tirch, D., Silberstein, L. R., & Kolts, R. L. (2015). *Buddhist psychology and cognitive-behavioral therapy: A clinician's guide*. NewYork, NY: Guilford Publications.

Torbert, W. R. (2004). *Action inquiry: The secret of timely and transforming leadership*. Oakland, CA: Berrett-Koehler Publishers.

Tsering, T. (2005). *The four noble truths: The foundation of Buddhist thought (vol. 1)*. New York, NY: Simon and Schuster.

Tsering, G. T. (2010). *Buddhist psychology: The foundation of Buddhist thought: Volume 3*. Boston, MA: Wisdom Publications.

Underhill, E. (2015). *Mysticism: A study in the nature and development of man's spiritual consciousness (vol. 8)*. London, England: Aeterna Press.

Van Schaik, S. (2011). *Tibet: A history*. New Haven, CT: Yale University Press.

Vøllestad, J., Nielsen, M. B., & Nielsen, G. H. (2012). Mindfulness-and acceptance-based interventions for anxiety disorders: A systematic review and meta-analysis. *British Journal of Clinical Psychology, 51*(3), 239-260.

Vygotsky, L. S. (1978). *Mind in society*. Cambridge, MA: Harvard University Press.

Wade, J. (1996). *Changes of mind: A holonomic theory of the evolution of consciousness*. Albany, NY: SUNY Press.

Wallace, A. (2007). *Contemplative science*. New York, NY: Columbia University Press.

Wangyal, R. T. (1998). *The Tibetan yoga of dream and sleep*. Ithaca, NY: Snow Lion Publications.

Wangyal, T. (2000). *Wonders of the natural mind: The essence of Rdzogchen in the native Bon tradition of Tibet*. Boston, MA: Shambhala Publications.

Washburn, M. (1988). *The ego and the dynamic ground: A transpersonal theory of human development*. Albany, NY: SUNY Press.

Washburn, M. (2000). Transpersonal cognition in developmental perspective. In K. Puhakka, P. Nelson, & T. Hart (Eds.), *Transpersonal knowing: Exploring the horizon of consciousness* (185-212). Albany, NY: SUNY Press.

Westen, D. (1998). The scientific legacy of Sigmund Freud: toward a psychodynamically informed psychological science. *Psychological Bulletin, 124*(3), p.333-371.

Westenberg, P. M. Blasi, A., & Cohn, L. D. (Eds.). (2013). *Personality development: Theoretical, empirical, and clinical investigations of Loevinger's conception of ego development.* New York, NY: Psychology Press.

Wilber, K., Engler, J., Brown, D. P., & Chirban, J. (1986). *Transformations of consciousness: Conventional and contemplative perspectives on development.* Boston, MA: New Science Library.

Wilber, K. (2000). *Integral psychology.* Boston, MA: Shambhala Publications.

Wilber, K. (2001) *Sex, ecology, spirituality: the spirit of evolution.* Boston, MA Shambhala Publications.

Wilber, K. (2007a). *Integral spirituality: A startling new role for religion in the modern and postmodern world.* Boston, MA: Shambhala Publications.

Wilber, K. (2007b). *A brief history of everything.* Boston, MA: Shambhala Publications.

Wilber, K. (2014). *The fourth turning: Imagining the evolution of an integral Buddhism.* Boston, MA: Shambhala Publications.

Wilber, K. (2017). The religion of tomorrow: A vision for the future of the great traditions. Boulder, CO: Shambhala Publications.

Witkiewitz, K., Bowen, S., Douglas, H., & Hsu, S. H. (2013). Mindfulness-based relapse prevention for substance craving. *Addictive Behaviors, 38*(2), 1563-1571.

World Health Organization. (2001). *Mental disorders.* Retrieved from www.who.int/whr/2001/media_centre/press_release/en/

Wells, A., & Purdon, C. (1999). Metacognition and cognitive-behaviour therapy: a special issue. *Clinical Psychology & Psychotherapy, 6*(2), 71-72.

Yates, J., Immergut, M., & Graves, J. (2017). *The mind illuminated: A complete meditation guide integrating Buddhist wisdom and brain science for greater mindfulness.* New York, NY: Simon and Schuster.

Yehuda, R., Engel, S. M., Brand, S. R., Seckl, J., Marcus, S. M., & Berkowitz, G. S. (2005). Transgenerational effects of posttraumatic stress disorder in babies of mothers exposed to the World Trade Center attacks during pregnancy. *The Journal of Clinical Endocrinology & Metabolism, 90*(7), 4115-4118.

Yogi, P. G. (2001). The Buddha. *Bulletin of Tibetology, 37*(1), 1-16.

Young-Eisendrath, P. (2008). The transformation of human suffering: A perspective from psychotherapy and Buddhism. *Psychoanalytic Inquiry, 28*(5), 541-549.

www.ingramcontent.com/pod-product-compliance
Lightning Source LLC
Chambersburg PA
CBHW071804090426
42737CB00012B/1951